John Davies was Bishop of Shrewsbury from 1987 to 1994. Previously, he spent many years in rural parish and city university ministry in South Africa, Wales and England. He is a former principal of the College of the Ascension in Birmingham and a Residentiary Canon of St Asaph Cathedral.

The author of numerous books and Bible study guides, he is now retired and lives near Llangollen, North Wales. He is a member of the local council, and with his wife Shirley is an associate of the Iona Community.

The Crisis of the Cross

The challenge at the heart
of the Christian story

John Davies

CANTERBURY
PRESS
Norwich

To Dr C F Beyers Naudé
Director of the Christian Institute of Southern Africa.
Leader of Christian witness in the struggle against apartheid.

© John Davies, 1997

First published in 1997 by The Canterbury Press Norwich
(a publishing imprint of Hymns Ancient & Modern Limited
a registered charity)
St Mary's Works, St Mary's Plain
Norwich, Norfolk NR3 3BH

All Bible quotations are taken from *The Dramatised Bible*,
by kind permission of the Bible Society.

British Library Cataloguing in Publication Data

A catalogue record for this book is available
from the British Library

ISBN 1-85311-190-2

Typeset by Rowland Phototypesetting
and printed and bound in Great Britain by
Biddles Ltd, Guildford and King's Lynn

Contents

Foreword
by the Archbishop of Wales

There are times when people find the Scriptures rather boring and inevitably dressed in archaic language.

Although we tend these days to describe the New Testament as a 'story' nevertheless, when read within the normal worship in the Church, the excitement of the occasion is very much absent.

In the mid-eighties Bishop John, during his assignment as Canon Missioner of St Asaph Cathedral, conducted Holy Week vigils for the young people of the diocese. One feature of these vigils, based on the passion stories from the Gospels, was to challenge the young people present to act parts of the story in public. In a fresh way this added to the excitement of listening to this dramatic event.

This collection of studies based on St John's Gospel are now published in order to show how exciting and dramatic the Gospel story can be.

Finally, I am pleased to acknowledge these studies on *The Crisis of the Cross* by Bishop John Dudley Davies as my Lent Book for 1998.

+ Alwyn Cambrensis

Alwyn Cambrensis
The Feast of St James 1997

Introduction

Once on a visit to Dublin, I was taken by some enterprising students to watch a sheep-judging competition. The aim of the competition was not to find the best sheep, but to find the best judges of sheep. The standards were rigorous and highly defined. I found myself wondering whether there were any similar standards which were applied to those who are in the business of judging people. This was a particularly sharp question for me, as I was beginning a period of several years in which I would be increasingly judging or assessing other people.

The headlines tell us constantly that there is a crisis – in government, in society, in international relations, in the Church. The word 'crisis' fundamentally means judgement, a moment when assessment has to be made, or, in our common phrase, a 'moment of truth'.

The theme of 'crisis' is one of the central ideas in the Gospel of John. Jesus comes as the light and the truth which expose and judge the darkness and the untruth within the world. This theme comes together most precisely in the story of the arrest, trials and crucifixion of Jesus. He is judged by the powers of religion, state and public opinion; in making their judgements about him they themselves are judged. He brings the crisis to those who judge him.

Now, Christians say that Jesus is our judge, and will come to be our judge. But his qualification to be our judge lies in this fact: that he has himself been judged. He has experienced the criticism and condemnation of the world and of religion. Therefore he identifies with those who are the victims of human judgement. Although he died a peculiarly horrible kind of death, it was, in fact, the result not of a massive and unique miscarriage of justice, but of a whole lot of pressures, mistakes, miscalculations and prejudices which are fairly understandable, and even commonplace, given the general mess of the world as we know it.

The Gospel of John was written for a group of Christians who were a small minority in society. They had good reason to feel very insecure and anxious about the meaning of their commitment and the reliability of their members. They were in a time of crisis. They treasured and recorded the Gospel stories, not just because these stories were interesting or profound in themselves, but because they were valuable tools for a community which had to give an account of itself and explain its character. That community would have to cope with questions like: What right have you to behave as you do? What right do you have to treat so casually the traditions of those who went before us? What right do you have to tell us that it makes no difference whether we are Jew or Gentile? Look at this so-called saviour of yours – he was a convicted blasphemer, so what right have you to tell us about religion? Look at this so-called king of yours – he was properly executed by the judicial authorities as a danger to public order; how do you then expect us to believe that you are not subversive also? Look at this so-called Christ of yours; how can you prove what you say about him? God didn't save him, and the Jews are still ground under the heel of the Roman imperialists, and the world is not better off; why should we let you go on confusing people with your senseless chatter? What's the use of a saviour who doesn't save, a king who doesn't rule, and a Christ who makes no noticeable difference? In response, the infant Church simply told its story. It said, 'This is Jesus; look at him. Look at him, and you find that if you try to judge him, he judges you. If you condemn him, you find that you are condemned.'

In following Jesus, our first predecessors in the Christian movement presented to the world the same crisis which Jesus had presented. The stories of the trials of Jesus gave them tools for understanding their own trials. The stories of the resurrection of Jesus helped them to realize the many different ways in which the new opportunity can be perceived by different people who follow the same Jesus. The first Christians knew very well what it was like to be infiltrated, to be betrayed by informers, to be the victims of prejudice, to be accused of disturbing the normal arrangements of society, to be punished without the proper legal process of charge, trial and conviction.

So we move to the present day. In many Christian communities today, these chapters of John's Gospel are the portions of Scripture which are set to be read at worship during Good Friday and Easter. The task of the preacher and worship leader is simply to let the story be heard, to allow it to make its own connections with our own time and place. This has been my task for 40 years, in a variety of local churches. These have included a barrack-room in a black mineworkers' compound in the Transvaal; mud-hut churches deep in South African rural areas; township churches around Johannesburg; town centre churches, country churches and cathedrals in Wales and England; study groups and conferences. I tried to put this preaching into written form in South Africa, in a booklet published by the Christian Institute; unusually for a book of Bible study, it was put under a banning order by the South African Government, under the Suppression of Communism Act.

This book has grown out of that work, in South Africa and Britain. I do not apologize for now offering to Britain a study which started in the South Africa of 30 to 40 years ago. It represents an opportunity for one church to learn something from the experience of another. There has been a massive flow of learning from British Christianity to African Christianity; here is a small example of a reverse flow. I have been particularly encouraged by the books of two bishop friends who have written commentaries on John's Gospel. To me, it is no accident that they both make deep use of their experience of other parts of the world. Lesslie Newbigin (*The Light has Come*) sees the Gospel against the background of his many years in India; Stephen Verney (*Water into Wine*) refers to his life with guerilla movements and shepherds in the Middle and Near East. We in South Africa felt that we had much to learn from the experience of the Confessing Church in Germany in the days of Hitler; one of the highlights of my time in South Africa was the visit of Martin Niemöller, who was a very special inspiration to us. At a time when everything was getting worse, when we were ruled and crushed by the ideology of apartheid and the machinery of a police state, we felt that we were a witnessing minority, called to be a confessing church. We were able to find many connections between our situation and the story told in these chapters of John's Gospel.

Wherever the Gospel is read, we are called to work out the connections between it and the situation which we are in, here and now. This is what readers and study groups are invited to do as they use this book. Sometimes these connections may be clear and relevant. For instance, I know only too well that almost any committed movement will have had the experience of coping with members who betray it or let it down. I have certainly broken the eucharistic bread with persons who have been, consciously or unconsciously, informers or agents of the Security Police. I have known occasions (including at least one in Britain), where the life of a Christian community has come to a standstill until I have taken part in the ejection of an informer. I have known how a small committed group has felt the need to protect itself and to lie to the authorities about its activities and its members, and I have contributed to that deceit myself. I have relied on the immense value of the rule of law: as a defendant, I have owed my acquittal to the principle that a magistrate will not hear the defence until the prosecution has made a coherent presentation of the case against the accused. I think that the only text of Scripture which I have carried on a placard in a public procession is: 'If I spoke amiss, state it in evidence; if I spoke wrong, why do you strike me?'

I have quoted these specimens of my own experience, because this is what I want to encourage readers of this book to do: I hope that they will make their own connections between the Gospel story and their own experience. This book is not intellectual speculation; with its limitations and its biases it has the authority of my experience. It is testimony. I want to encourage readers and study groups to claim a similar authority.

So, in the past, I have personally found many immediate parallels between the text and my own circumstances. But circumstances change. For the Church in present-day South Africa, the question has to be: what does a Church which is 'at ease' with the State have to learn from its previous experience of being in opposition to it? For the Church in Germany, the question would be: how does the Church as a whole learn from 40 years' experience of the Church in East Germany? And similarly, what does the present German Church – or, for that matter, the whole of European Christianity – have to learn from the experience of the Confessing Church in Germany during the days of Nazi power? Those in Britain who try to tell the Church to keep out of political issues are asking us to unlearn the most painful and expensive lessons which Christianity has had to learn in Europe in this century.

Britain still has much to learn about these issues, both as a Church and as a group of nations. Apartheid was, of course, a uniquely South African heresy, but its political structures were in many ways shaped by decisions made earlier in this century in Britain. Even during its decline it was propped up by powerful interests in this country. More importantly, many of the underlying motives and spiritual bases of apartheid are alive and well among us in Britain to this day, and these need to be faced with the judgement – the crisis – of the Gospel. We define people in terms of where they come from; we label people according to features such as gender or racial origin, features which normally cannot be changed and over which the individual has no control; and these features have real power, for instance in employment. We maintain patterns of privilege which make some people second-class citizens in their own country. We need to have a group of people to whom we can feel superior, whom we can laugh at, whom we can blame, whom we can reckon as failures. These are some of the building-blocks of racism, and they are all around us as we try to sort out our relationship with Ireland, our treatment of Jews, our receiving of new communities since 1945, and our attitudes to Europe.

We may, perhaps, put our confidence in the ideal of 'One Nation', and hope for the disappearance of the old divide between middle class and working class; but in our modern state the real divide is between all the working classes on the one hand, and the non-working class on the other. The latter is the class of the homeless, the unemployed, the disabled; they are pushed further and further away from the so-called mainstream of our society – the employed, the possessors, and the army of consultants, advisors, planners and trainers whose livelihood depends on the continued existence of the non-working class. We elevate 'self-fulfilment' as an ideal to be aimed at by each individual; we measure that self-fulfilment in terms of how many things we possess and how long the distances we travel. Then we have to increase our policing to combat the vandalism and violence of people who feel that they have no other form of self-fulfilment. The structures of our political system force even idealistic politicians to pay most attention to getting the votes of 'Middle England'. We should simply ask: 'Where would Jesus fit into our electoral pro-gramme?' Surely he would be closest to those who get least advantage from all our systems, because that is where he is to be found in the Gospel – treated as unnecessary to the State, embarrassing to religion and redundant to the general public.

Our religious institutions must come under similar judgement. Often they seem to be more concerned with survival than with transformation, and they connive with our yearning to identify people on whom to fix the blame for our national ills. Our churches appear to be strangely uninterested in the precious value of the rule of law – in a State where a would-be immigrant can be detained for years while investigations are made, and where accused persons can be remanded in custody for many long months before eventually being brought to trial. Now, many of us probably do not feel that we are in a police state, but many apparently benign organizations (including churches) have a kind of security police, which make people feel that they are under surveillance.

I am sure that many people would say that this is all exaggeration, that life is not like that. But in South Africa white people would write to the papers, declaring that they could not understand what the fuss was all about – 'I have never felt that I am in a police state', they would say. And the answer has to be: you are showing how far away you are from the experience of most of the inhabitants of your country. We need to check how far we know something of the experience of those people who are most disadvantaged in our society. All too often the people who make the decisions which affect unemployed or homeless people have never themselves known what it is like to be unemployed or homeless. Can you solve a situation which you have not shared? The Gospel tells us that the Son of God was incarnated among us, that he put himself at the mercy of the place where he belonged. He descended to the bottom of a society which treated him as valueless and redundant – he ended up in the dregs. The Gospel tells us that the Son of God is found on the wrong side of human systems of religion, law and public opinion. He is our great priest because he has been the victim, and that is where his followers are called to be.

As we look at the various characters, roles and experiences in the story told by John, I think that we shall find that they have their counterparts and connections in any society which we care to name. Just as I have seen links between the Gospel story and the South Africa of 30 years ago, so I am sure that there are many parallels with our situation in this country now. I have been assured of this whenever I have tried to explore the story in this way in recent years.

I am overwhelmingly indebted to the many different people with whom I have worked on this text over the years. They will have to be nameless, although I have mentioned some groups of them already. The theory which underlies this way of preaching on Good Friday is set out convincingly in Canon John Fenton's two short books, *Preaching the Cross* and *The Passion According to John*.

John Davies
Froncysyllte, Wales
Ascension Day 1997

How to Use this Book

This book is intended to help Christians use the Gospel story as a way of renewing their faith and discipleship. In this way it is intended to serve the same purpose for which the Gospel itself was written. The essential task for readers, whether working alone or with others, is to let the story make its own connections with their own experience and their own situation. No one else can do this for us. You are the expert on your own situation. All that a book like this can do is to offer a few hints. Any programme which is too rigid might get in the way. The questions which I am offering are only suggestions; don't be dominated by them. Use them if you find them helpful, but don't duck them simply to avoid awkward arguments! The most important questions, however, will be the questions which come out of your own situation.

Group Work

The best way of handling this book for group study would be for each member to read a chapter or part of a chapter in preparation for the meeting. At the meeting the set passage should be read aloud – preferably with different people taking different parts in the storytelling and dialogue. (The excellent tradition of reading the Passion story in parts on Palm Sunday and Good Friday has been made much easier by the publication of *The Dramatised Bible.*) Then members can give their own answers to the general questions which follow each chapter, moving on to more specific ones which arise out of that particular section of the story.

Much of the story has to do with the processes of judgement. Do not assume that this is relevant only for people who are, in some professional sense, judges. Rightly or wrongly, we are constantly passing judgement on others: children do so on each other and on adults; parents, teachers and neighbours do so, as well as administrators, employers, the police, lawyers, church councillors and ministers. As we read this story, we should find that all our conventional ways of making judgements are put under scrutiny.

The underlying question for us, as followers of Jesus, in our own day, has to be this:

If this is what happened when God was present in the world in the person of Jesus of Nazareth, how is God present in the Body of Christ now? What is the meaning of this story for our obedience in the Church today? How do we share in the conflicts and the resurrection of Jesus now?

Perhaps your group could appoint someone to act as note-taker, not to make a detailed report but to record points which might be worth assembling at the end of your work with this book, for passing on to other people (see the note at the end of the 'For Group Work' section of chapter 6).

The Prayers

I have supplied some suggestions for prayer after each chapter. These are prayers and reflections which I happen to find useful. I have found it difficult to select them out of the immense range of prayers new and old, which have been inspired by the central story of the Gospel. So, if you find them helpful, fine. If not, don't be bound by them. Whatever you do, don't use these prayers, or any other prayers, just as a quick spiritual flip before going home. Give time to your praying. Allow space, and more space. Use words in prayer only when you have to; the silence may be much more truly a way into closeness with God.

1

Arrest

Jesus' arrest

John 18:1–13

Narrator   Jesus left with his disciples and went across the brook called Kidron. There was a garden in that place, and Jesus and his disciples went in. Judas, the traitor, knew where it was, because many times Jesus had met there with his disciples. So Judas went to the garden, taking with him a group of Roman soldiers, and some temple guards sent by the chief priests and the Pharisees: they were armed and carried lanterns and torches. Jesus knew everything that was going to happen to him, so he stepped forward [and asked them:]

Jesus   Who is it you are looking for?

Soldier 1   Jesus of Nazareth.

Jesus   I am he.

Narrator   Judas, the traitor, was standing there with them. When Jesus said to them, 'I am he,' they moved back and fell to the ground. Again Jesus asked them:

Jesus   Who is it you are looking for?

Soldier 2   Jesus of Nazareth.

Jesus   I have already told you that I am he. If, then, you are looking for me, let these others go.

Narrator   He said this so that what he had said might come true: 'Father, I have not lost even one of those you gave me.'

Simon Peter, who had a sword, drew it and struck the High Priest's slave, cutting off his right ear. The name of the slave was Malchus. [Jesus said to Peter:]

Jesus   Put your sword back in its place! Do you think that I will not drink the cup of suffering which my Father has given me?

Narrator   Then the Roman soldiers with their commanding officer and the Jewish guards arrested Jesus, bound him, and took him away.

This is the story of the final crisis of the life of Jesus. It is the final confrontation between Jesus and the powers of darkness. Jesus meets the destructiveness of the world face to face.

It all starts on Jesus' home ground. The garden is the regular meeting-place for Jesus and his colleagues. It is not their workplace – that is the temple and the frontier post; rather, it is the place of their evening gathering. It is the place of the night; and the night, in John's story, is the time when work ceases. The arrest follows the same tactic as a police dawn raid – it happens in a place of familiarity and relaxation.

This is the story of the handing over of Jesus. First of all, Jesus is handed over by Judas. Judas and his actions have become immensely important in the Christian story. At every Eucharist, of whatever tradition, the eucharistic action is carried out to recall what happened 'in the same night when he was betrayed'. Judas has been marvellously analysed in drama and opera and imagery of every kind. But the arrest and trials and crucifixion of Jesus could have happened without him; organizationally, he was scarcely necessary to the police action. Why, then, is he given such importance in the story?

Surely because this is the story of the confrontation between the representative of God and the powers of darkness; and whenever the representatives of God, however inadequately, get involved in any contemporary form of this confrontation, they will face the problem of one of their own number acting as informer. There will be the ambitious disciple, the one who tries to be on both sides at once. Judas has shared in the fellowship-meal; he has taken part in the inner life of the little community. The community may be aware that one of them will betray, but they do not know who. So our eucharistic fellowship is constantly reminded that it is in a betraying world, that its life is lived in a betraying environment. The community of Jesus is not secure against internal betrayal; the Judas story assures us that it never has been. Each of us may need to ask, 'Is it I?' But the Gospel tells us that this capacity for betrayal is all part of the disorder which Jesus has met and mastered in the cross.

The informer, while having some accurate information for which someone may be willing to pay, is deeply ignorant. He is of the darkness. The system of evil is incorrigibly and eternally stupid. Judas, in spite of those months and years of companionship with Jesus, assumes that Jesus will defend himself with physical force; so he collects an enormous squad of 600 armed men. He assumes that Jesus will hide, so he ignores the fact that there will be the full moon of the Passover, and arranges for plenty of artificial light. He sees Jesus as the universal enemy, so he organizes an arresting party drawn from the widest possible range of sources – soldiers from the Roman garrison, officials from the religious establishment, representatives of the Pharisees, the moral enthusiasts. These all fall in behind Judas, sinking their differences in their common opposition to the truth that is in Jesus. They are led by this follower of Jesus, who now follows Jesus down the long descent from the city into the secluded and familiar garden.

And yet all this elaborate and expensive operation is entirely unnecessary. Jesus himself takes the initiative. He has no need to be hunted. He comes forward to meet this miscellaneous army. He asks them whom they are seeking. He requires them to state their purpose. They answer 'Jesus of Nazareth' – Jesus, from that disreputable, provincial, distant village. In spite of the full moon, in spite of their lanterns and torches, in spite of the informer's personal knowledge, they do not identify Jesus until he identifies himself. In spite of all their artificial equipment, in spite of the strength of their contrived alliance, Jesus acts first, speaks first and retains control of events. The hardware with which they equip themselves is just useless ironmongery. Energy used against Jesus is sheer waste.

Jesus answers, 'I am he.' A simple statement; but the reader of the Gospel will know that this is nothing less than the name of God – the I AM of the Exodus, the Passover deliverance. Several times earlier in the Gospel, Jesus has used this special phrase about some aspect of his identity and nature: I AM the Bread of life, I AM the Good Shepherd, and so on. Now he uses it finally and simply – 'I AM.'

It knocks them down; they cannot stand before this revelation of the divine glory in the man who simply acknowledges the truth about himself. All that they can do is to repeat his name: 'Jesus of Nazareth'. They make no further move until he has arranged for the security of his disciples. He does not wish that they be led into the place of temptation. He himself has to go forward into the confrontation, but there is no need for the rest of his community to be drawn into it. Earlier he had called these men to follow him; now he orders that they should be free.

There is a second betrayer amongst the disciples. Peter has not taken up the kind of deliberate commitment which led Judas into the darkness, but he is the blind, stupid one who betrays what Jesus is standing for. He uses the world's weapons to oppose the world. He tries to protect Jesus. But Jesus wants and needs no such protection. So Peter finds himself standing up for no one except himself. He draws the sword which, without permission, he has brought with him. He attacks Malchus, not an armed soldier or trained policeman, but the defenceless slave of the High Priest, one who has not chosen to be there and is not even paid to be there, but who is merely a slave obeying orders. The Gospel writer insists that even such an insignificant person is an individual with a name and an identity. But for Peter, Malchus is just a body to lash out at, a safe target. He acts in a way which is exactly the opposite to that of the Christ who opened the ears of the deaf and cared for the weak and insignificant. Peter is the man of vigour and zeal; he has some qualifications for becoming a senior church leader. But when the church leader loses touch with Christ, and does not know where Christ is going, he can do more damage than Christ's avowed enemies. No one lost an ear on account of Judas. Malchus stands as the test for the vigorous, active and enthusiastic Church. It is not in business to hurt the ignorant and puzzled who happen to be on the wrong side. It is not called to lash out at those who simply find themselves serving the one tradition which they know. It may not protect itself or its Master by using the world's weapons of destruction. Jesus says, 'Put your weapons back where they can do no more damage; I have things to do which are more important than survival.'

Christ breaks things and sees things on original personality. He knows us truthfully.

For Group Work

General Questions

- How does this story fit into my experience?

- What bells does it ring for me?

- Have I ever been in the same situation as one of the characters in the story?

Specific Questions

1 How does the story of Judas fit into your experience?

2 'In the same night that he was betrayed...' Almost all churches use this phrase at the heart of the central prayer of the Eucharist or Holy Communion. Our worship calls us to realize that we worship in a world where betrayal is all around us. Some people are betrayed by other individuals; others feel betrayed by big organizations which fail to deliver: for example, political parties, councils, the Health Service, banks and building societies, employers, providers of services, the Church. How do we bring our experiences of a cruel world into our worship? Could you ask the person who usually presides at the Eucharist to say what this phrase means to him/her, as pastor and minister?

3 Is your church truly on the side of the weak and powerless, or does it help to make them victims of cruelty or scorn (the Malchus question)?

For Prayer

Lord Christ, Lamb of God, Lord of Lords,
call us, who are called to be saints,
  along the way of your cross.
Draw us, who would draw near to our King,
  to the foot of your cross.
Cleanse us, who are not worthy to approach,
  with the pardon of your cross.
Instruct us, the ignorant and blind,
  in the school of your cross.
Arm us, for the battles of holiness,
  with the might of your cross.
Bring us, in the fellowship of your sufferings,
  to the victory of your cross.
And seal us, in the kingdom of your glory,
  among the servants of your cross.
O crucified Lord,
  risen Saviour. Amen.

From *My God My Glory*, E. Milner-White, adapted

O Christ, the Master Carpenter, who at the last, through wood and nails, purchased our whole salvation; wield well your tools in the workshop of your world, so that we who come rough-hewn to your bench may here be fashioned to a truer beauty of your hand. We ask it for your own name's sake. Amen.

From the *Iona Community Worship Book*

2

False and Genuine Security

Peter denies Jesus

John 18:12–27

Narrator The Roman soldiers with their commanding officer and the Jewish guards arrested
Jesus and bound him. They took him first
to Annas. He was the father-in-law of Caiaphas, who was High Priest that year. It
was Caiaphas who had advised the Jewish
authorities that it was better that one man
should die for all the people.
Simon Peter and another disciple followed
Jesus. That other disciple was well-known
to the High Priest, so he went with Jesus into
the courtyard of the High Priest's house,
while Peter stayed outside by the gate. Then
the other disciple went back out, spoke to
the girl at the gate, and brought Peter inside.
The girl at the gate said to Peter:

Girl (to Peter)	Aren't you also one of the disciples of that man?
Peter	No, I am not.
Narrator	It was cold, so the servants and guards had built a charcoal fire and were standing round it, warming themselves. So Peter went over and stood with them, warming himself. (PAUSE)
	The High Priest questioned Jesus about his disciples and about his teaching. Jesus answered:
Jesus	I have always spoken publicly to everyone; all my teaching was done in the synagogues and in the Temple, where all the people come together. I have never said anything in secret. Why, then, do you question me? Question the people who heard me. Ask them what I told them – they know what I said.
Narrator	When Jesus said this, one of the guards there slapped him:
Guard	How dare you talk like that to the High Priest!
Jesus	If I have said anything wrong, tell everyone here what it was. But if I am right in what I have said, why do you hit me?
Narrator	Then Annas sent him, still bound, to Caiaphas the High Priest. (PAUSE)
	Peter was still standing there keeping himself warm. [So the others said to him:]
Person 1 (to Peter)	Aren't you also one of the disciples of that man?

Narrator	But Peter denied it:
Peter	No, I am not.
Narrator	One of the High Priest's slaves, a relative of the man whose ear Peter had cut off, spoke up.
Person 2 (to Peter)	Didn't I see you with him in the garden?
Peter	No!
Narrator	And at once a cock crowed.

Jesus ensures the freedom of the disciple-community. He also secures the freedom of the poor and weak from being the victim of the disciple's self-interest. Now he is ready to relinquish his own freedom. He submits to being arrested and handcuffed.

Annas is Jesus' first interrogator. He is the ex-president of the religious conference, the High Priest, the elder statesman whose opinion cannot be ignored. Legally, he had been deposed from office by the pagan state; true believers would regard this as improper interference, and they would count continued recognition of Annas as a sign of defiant loyalty to the religious authority. But Caiaphas is the legally recognized High Priest in the eyes of the Government. He is the shrewd establishment man, who has advised that social stability is worth the death of one individual. Who would say that he was wrong? Of course, Caiaphas is unjust; but would he be less unjust if he allowed public unrest to develop, which would bring many more deaths at the hand of a nervous and trigger-happy foreign governor?

The death of Jesus is the result of a typical situation in

which all courses of action are relatively unsatisfactory. More people suffer as a result of this sort of moral ambiguity than from blatant injustice. The question of Caiaphas is always, 'Yes, but what is the alternative?' Jesus dies because he refuses compromise. His resurrection is a victory over the daily erosion of morals, as well as being a victory over the catastrophic powers of cosmic darkness. It is this victory, which Caiaphas, with unconscious prophetic insight, foretells. Whether he likes it or not, he is an agent of the divine communication system. He speaks the truth; Christ will die for the people. This is victory for Christ's purpose. But it is defeat for Caiaphas' purpose, because Jesus is redefining 'the people'. For Caiaphas, 'the people' is the national and religious in-group, defined by ancestry and tradition; for Caiaphas, God's interests coincide with the nation's political necessity. But Jesus is the Good Shepherd who will draw people together across boundaries of nationality and religious background. Through his death he will attract people into a new 'people', in which the old exclusive insignia will no longer have the power to separate. Jesus sets us free from Caiaphas' definition of 'the people'. If we claim Christ as support for our own idea of 'people' – nation, Church, race, family, culture or morality – then we revert to Caiaphas; our contribution will be part of the world's tragedy, not of its hope. When we draw a line between ourselves and other groups, we find that Jesus is on the far side of that line.

Our Evangelist is like the scriptwriter of a soap opera. He switches back and forth between each scene, updating them in turn, playing off one against another. So we go back to Peter. Christ is the servant of the truth, in confrontation with the institutionalized powers of darkness, represented by political and religious authority. Peter is the isolated disciple who fails to take Christ's Word seriously and who seeks a phoney security detached from Christ. The Church has these two options to choose from; the story spells out the implications of that choice.

Earlier in the Gospel story, Peter had been told to follow, and did so. But now he has been given a different order – he has been sent home – and he cannot adapt himself to this new, unspectacular instruction. He insists on continuing to follow. So he finds himself in the place of danger and insecurity, without the companionship of Jesus. He is determined to stay in the picture, despite the fact that his one piece of equipment, his sword, has been declared to be useless. The keen but disobedient disciple makes very little difference to the eventual outcome, but he has considerable 'nuisance value'. Because he is out of touch with the instructions of Christ, he is motivated by the demands of his own self-image and finds himself acting as an alien to the truth.

Peter is abetted by 'another disciple'. This disciple is given no name, but he is most probably the anonymous and significant figure who elsewhere is called 'the disciple whom Jesus loved' and 'the disciple who wrote these things'. But here he is not called 'the beloved disciple', he is called 'the disciple who was known to the High Priest'. He has contacts, so he is able to get into the courtyard. There, he feels embarrassed by the fact that his friend is out in the cold, so he uses his influence to bring Peter in. He leads Peter straight into the place of temptation, falsity and downfall. It is dangerous to trade on one's influence with the enemies of Jesus. If one is not known by the name of Jesus – 'the disciple whom Jesus loved' – one must be known by the name of the enemy: 'the one who was known to the High Priest'. So disciple leads disciple into temptation.

It needs a strong shepherd to keep the door of the sheep; a teenage girl is sufficient for the High Priest's courtyard. She keeps the door. She need ask only one question, and this question does not require a bully or an investigator or a captain of the Security Police to put it: 'Surely you're not one of this man's disciples as well?' (that is, as well as this other disciple, about whom we know already). She makes it easy for him to say 'No'. And he says 'No.' Jesus, the truth, in response to the challenge to his identity, says 'I am'; Peter, in response to the challenge to his identity, says 'I am not.' I am not a disciple. I have no relationship with Jesus. I am not.

Peter is out of the companionship of Jesus. He joins the community of cold and darkness, the servants and officers who depend on an artificial source of warmth to keep comfortable. So he also separates himself from the disciple who has taken the trouble to get him admitted to the courtyard. He cannot deny Jesus and still stay with Jesus' friend; the only place left for him is with Jesus' enemies.

Peter's denial is not just a matter of simple cowardice. He has got where he is because of his personal courage, independence of mind and commitment to Jesus. He still has a weapon, and would be ready to use it. His denial

is good common sense. When the leader of our movement is under arrest, we will surely do our best to keep
as close to him as we can; we will be economical with
the truth in order to preserve our freedom of action and
to safeguard our colleagues. We are under no obligation
to give accurate information to our enemies. Many
honourable members of resistance movements have had
to take this line. But Jesus does not want to be protected
or rescued. His way of saving is not the way of common
sense or heroic courage. Peter's 'I am not' is the sign of
his failure to see, and to work with, Christ's unique way
of healing the world's disease. So, like Caiaphas, Peter
is the continuing question to the methods and the vision
of the movement which claims to follow Jesus.

From this scene of darkness and cold, we move back
again to the place of the central confrontation, where
Jesus faces the real enemy. Annas is the power of prejudice. He is not conducting a case in court; he does not
follow the legal requirement for accusations to be sup-
ported by the evidence of witnesses – he acts as his own
investigator. He does not want evidence, he wants only
confirmation of his prejudice, so he acts as prosecutor
without witnesses and without judge. He does not ask
about Jesus' actions; he concentrates on Jesus' associates
and utterances, which are more likely to be incriminating.

But under the Jewish law of those days (just as under
our own law), it was contrary to the rule of law for an
accused person to be coerced into incriminating himself.
So Jesus replies by pointing out the lack of any need to
bypass the normal processes of hearing evidence. 'I have

always spoken in public. There has never been anything secret or underhand about my work. You do not have to take my word for it. You can get all the information you want from those who have heard me.' Jesus refuses to co-operate with the device of a private investigation. He demands a public trial with proper evidence. He has not trained his disciples to behave like a secret conspiracy. He refuses to make a neat summary of his teaching. The time for teaching has passed and, in any case, he has not formulated a creed; from now on, his teaching will consist of whatever has made sense to his disciples and has lodged in their memory. It will now be their responsibility to communicate on Jesus' behalf. He has left no writings, no video or tape recordings. People can know of Jesus only through his friends. To those who are eager to discover what Jesus really thought, or what he really would have done, there is only one response: ask those who have heard – they know. So, ask the Sunday congregation, ask the baptized children, ask the church stewards – they will tell you; it's their job. And it's our job, not only to answer the friendly enquirer, but to answer Annas.

Jesus is insisting on the proper processes of law, which ought to be perfectly acceptable. But this court is not governed by the rational rule of law, it is governed by prejudice; and this prejudice has passed infectiously from president to policeman. How dare the prisoner attempt to instruct the president of the court in legal procedure? This is a cheeky prisoner; he needs to be put in his place. So, one bending of the rules leads to another, and violence takes over. When the authoritarian person finds himself in the wrong, he tries to put things right by getting deeper into wrong. He resorts to some sort of physical or structural or social violence. This is the weakness of the law; even if it were a perfect system, it cannot always control its own agents. Further, Annas and his police are not the supreme autocrats of the world. They are voteless non-citizens, men who in the eyes of the real power bearers of the Roman Empire are irritating natives playing little power games. The relatively poor and powerless are not immune from the temptation of prejudice and injustice.

Jesus, the prisoner, upholds the law in the face of the law's agents. He presents them with a crisis. The policeman seeks to assert the authority of the law by overriding the law's standards. He treats an unconvicted prisoner as if he had already been found guilty. He deals Jesus a slap on the face, with the words, 'So that's how you speak to the High Priest, is it?' Jesus' reply is the classic response of non-violence, which has served as a model answer among the first Christian communities and in so many similar situations ever since: 'If I have spoken amiss, produce evidence to prove it. If not, why do you strike me?'

Jesus has committed himself to positive non-violence and voluntary powerlessness. This incites a response which does violence not only to himself, but to the whole rule of law. Jesus shows himself as the one who is alongside all who are treated to this kind of injustice. He stands for the value and validity of the law, which, in so far as it is *just* law, mirrors the justice of God. In his non-violence, he is the wielder of true authority; in his powerlessness, he is the one with true power. Annas has nothing more that he can contribute after this. He concludes the hearing.

We leave Jesus to be taken before Caiaphas, and return to the dark, cold courtyard. Jesus' hands are tied; Peter's hands are free to stretch out to the fire. His denial has taken the heat off him; he can enjoy the warmth of the burning charcoal. But not for long. The girl's original question is picked up by others who have their suspicions. He denies it again: 'I am not.' But now his earlier actions have their consequence. He is recognized by a relative of the poor slave Malchus; this brings a quite specific and verifiable identification: 'Didn't I see you with him in the garden?' This could be disastrous. It could lead to prosecution for assault and attempting to obstruct the course of justice; it could lead to revenge from Malchus' family; it could get the whole disciple-community into deep trouble. So he can scarcely avoid a third denial. 'No, you did not see me in the garden. You may perhaps have seen a disciple of Jesus there: a man called Peter. But that is not me. I have nothing in common with him. For all I know, he does not exist. Do not ask me who I am. All I can say is that I am not.'

The Gospel writer does not ask us to enter into the emotions of Peter. He simply puts Peter's story before us. This little tragedy of one person's conscience has its place within the cosmic drama of salvation. It is part of the personal history of the best-known member of the community of disciples. It is the sort of experience which can crop up at any time within the life of the movement which is committed to the continuing purpose of Jesus in the world. So we should not be surprised if we see the story being repeated in our own experience; it is still part of the programme of salvation. By the time the story was written in the form in which we receive it, Peter was known throughout the Church as a chief leader of the movement, a senior apostle. The story of his denials was not suppressed. It continues to pose a pertinent question to those who want to be sure of the blamelessness and virtuousness of designated Church leaders. On any reasonable assessment, Peter would not seem to be a suitable candidate for such leadership; his qualifications scarcely inspire confidence. (Even when he became a trusted leader, he still seems to have been the kind of character who couldn't take anything on board until it was knocked into his head three times in quick succession.) The one thing which makes him worthy as a Church leader is that he has been recon-structed by Jesus, and that is sufficient.

But this is for the future. For now, Peter has no more part in the story. Jesus and Peter are committed in oppo-site directions. They will not meet again until there is the new creation in the resurrection. In denying Jesus Peter has been denying himself; he is not crucified, but has consigned himself into non-existence.

A major part of the crisis has reached a climax. The community to which Jesus belongs by ancestry and religious tradition has rejected him. He has been denied by the leader of his own group of special colleagues. He is now completely on his own, and there is no one from whom he can expect support or sympathy.

The cock crows. Jesus moves away from the niggling domestic preoccupations of the local religious authorities to face the representative of the greatest and noblest secular power in the world, the power of imperial Rome.

For Group Work

General Questions

- How does this story fit into my experience?

- What bells does it ring for me?

- Have I ever been in the same situation as one of the characters in the story?

Specific Questions

1 How does the story of Peter fit into your experience?

2 How does the story of Annas and Caiaphas fit into your experience?

3 Look at the way your church, school or religious group deals with people when accusations, complaints or grumbles are made against them. Does it behave with strict justice? Does it ensure a fair hearing? Is it an example to other groups?

4 What do you think are the qualifications for a
church leader? Could you get a church leader to
reflect on the story of Peter with you?

For Prayer

*Think again of the stories of the religious leaders,
Annas and Caiaphas. Think again of the story of the
leading disciple and chief apostle, Peter. Pray for the
Church, local and worldwide.*

Lord God,
Forgive your church:
Its silence when called to speak;
Its failure to speak with your voice;
Its wealth among the poor;
Its cowardice among the oppressed;
Its confusion in standing for the truth.
Forgive us, your people:
Our lack of confidence in your presence with us;
Our lack of hope in the coming of your kingdom;
Our lack of interest in the sufferings of your world.
Forgive us, your servants:
When we isolate our leaders,
When we complain without meeting,
When we tolerate misunderstandings,
When we ignore the calling of our comrades.
Lord, take us;

Lord, break us;
Lord, remake us.
Amen.

*A prayer to Christ, who has been with us through
the conflict with the evil of the world, and is alive to
be alongside us.*

Risen Jesus,
you are there close beside each person,
you descend to where we are,
to the very lowest point of our human condition,
and you take upon yourself all that hurts us,
both in ourselves and in others.
You accompany every human being.
More than that,
you visit even those who, as non-believers,
have died without being able to know you.
And so, in our inner struggle,
the contemplation
gives rise to a radiant goodness
in the humble heart that allows itself to be led
by your Spirit.

Prayer of Brother Roger of Taizé

3

Truth and Subversion

Jesus is brought before Pilate

John 18:28–40

Narrator Early in the morning Jesus was taken from Caiaphas' house to the governor's palace. The Jewish authorities did not go inside the palace, for they wanted to keep themselves ritually clean, in order to be able to eat the Passover meal. So Pilate went outside to them:

Pilate What do you accuse this man of?

Priest We would not have brought him to you if he had not committed a crime.

Pilate Then you yourselves take him and try him according to your own law.

Person 1 We are not allowed to put anyone to death. (PAUSE)

Narrator	Pilate went back into the palace and called Jesus.
Pilate	Are you the King of the Jews?
Narrator	Jesus answered:
Jesus	Does this question come from you or have others told you about me?
Pilate	Do you think I am a Jew? It was your own people and the chief priests who handed you over to me. What have you done?
Jesus	My kingdom does not belong to this world; if my kingdom belonged to this world, my followers would fight to keep me from being handed over to the Jewish authorities. No, my kingdom does not belong here!
Pilate	Are you a king, then? (PAUSE)
Jesus	You say that I am a king. I was born and came into the world for this one purpose, to speak about the truth. Whoever belongs to the truth listens to me.
Pilate (slowly)	And what is truth? (PAUSE)
Narrator	Then Pilate went back outside to the people.
Pilate	I cannot find any reason to condemn him. But according to the custom you have, I always set free a prisoner for you during the Passover. Do you want me to set free for you the King of the Jews?
Person 1	No, not him!
Person 2	We want Barabbas!

Narrator Barabbas was a bandit (PAUSE)
(slowly)

'Cock crow' is a technical term in the army's timetable. It is the time for the changing of the guard from the third to the fourth watch of the night, and for the commencement of the phase of the day called 'early'. In this story, cock crow is the moment when Jesus comes under a new administration; his case is transferred to Pilate.

'*They* led Jesus . . .'; '*They* did not enter the praetorium'; '*They* answered . . .' The members of the anti-Jesus conspiracy have become anonymous. They have no identity except in their desire to get rid of him. But there are limits to what they will do. They will not contaminate themselves by going into the pagan Governor's house; they will not run the risk of being unable to take part in the annual celebration of their national liberation. But they have no such scruples about trying to manipulate the Governor into condemning and executing the Messiah.

The Governor has to decide how far he is going to allow himself to be manipulated by those whom he is supposed to rule; anyone who has held any kind of authority will sympathize with him in this problem. As we shall see, he does have deeper problems about truth and justice. But he is also vulnerable politically. He is in the classic position of a man who holds all the formal power, while all around him are people who are deprived of power but who want to get out of him what they can. Where a community has no political rights and no recognized political leadership, it may well try to use religion as a way of asserting itself. If it is blessed with people of courage and integrity, it may find a Tutu to speak for it; or it may find a Caiaphas. The Christian communities for whom the Evangelist wrote would urgently need to have an answer to the question, 'What kind of sympathy and what kind of justice can we expect from the unbelieving secular State?' The powerful and dramatic story in this Gospel, of the dialogue between Jesus and Pilate, would provide an answer to that question.

Pilate stands for the rule of law. It is his job to administer this law impartially, as one of the benefits given by imperial Rome to its subject nations. But he is also supposed to be keeping order over a particularly irritating and unpredictable subject nation, where communal disturbances could boil up at any time. So he knows that law and order do not necessarily go together. Keeping order may sometimes mean bending the law. In any case, the law was worked out by and for the benefit of the respectable Latin-speaking citizens of the imperial centre, and non-citizens could not assume that they had the right to share in all its privileges.

Pilate, in no mood for wasting time on courtesies, gets up long before normal office hours to meet the nationalist religious leaders. He demands to be told the charge against Jesus. This is the first responsibility of the magistrate; anyone who has been a defendant knows how important it is to ensure that the accusation is correctly framed. If the magistrate cannot understand exactly what it is that the defendant is accused of, the prosecution should fail. In this case, the accusers of Jesus think that the bare fact that they have taken the trouble to apprehend him ought to be sufficient proof that he is a criminal. 'We know right from wrong; you can trust us not to accuse an innocent person.' This is the voice of total commitment to a cause. We must be right, because we are going to such lengths, incurring so much expense, causing so much disruption and suffering – if what we are doing causes so much trouble, how can we possibly be wrong!

Pilate has no time for this kind of arm twisting. Between him and Jesus' accusers there is almost total non-communication. 'If you can't even mount a proper charge, don't bring me into it – you can deal with him on your own.' The accusers reply: 'Oh no, this is not just a little domestic matter, of the kind which you allow us to handle. This is a matter for the highest authority in the world. Our little local law is inadequate to deal with it. Only you have got the necessary powers and procedures, and that is what we want.'

Caiaphas had seen that one man might have to die for the nation. But Jesus does not die only for that nation; he does not undergo the local, tribal Jewish method of execution by stoning. He dies by the method recognized all over the Empire as the universal form of execution meted out by the Empire's courts: namely, crucifixion. He dies as a victim of the world's best and most widely respected system of justice.

Pilate moves back into his office, and calls Jesus in for interview. He can assume that an accused man will not be as worried about contamination as the accusers are. Indeed, Jesus has not been at all worried about where to go and whom to mix with; this is not the first time that he has entered a Gentile's house. He is going to die for Pilate and all other Gentiles; he will not object to spending some of his last hours in Gentile property. He obeys Pilate's summons. He is not interested in defiance for the sake of defiance.

Pilate's law, like Jewish law, requires that there should be a proper presentation of evidence by witnesses before the accused is convicted. The accused is not supposed to be convicted merely on his own unsubstantiated confession. Therefore, Pilate conducts a preliminary examination in private, which would, if he judges that there is a case to answer, lead to a proper hearing with witnesses.

Pilate is clear about his own terms of reference. He is not concerned with tribal religious questions, only with the authority of the state and the preservation of public order. So he focuses his enquiry upon the question of whether Jesus has any political ambitions. His first words are ambiguous: they may be a question – 'Are you the King of the Jews?'; or they could be a kind of statement – 'So you *are* the King of the Jews, are you?' Whatever Pilate means, Jesus takes his words and turns them back on him. He exercises the proper rights of an accused person; he needs to know the charge and the source of the evidence for it. 'Is what you are saying based on your own observation or on hearsay?' This is a proper question to put to Pilate as an officer of the law. But, at the same time, Jesus is speaking to Pilate as a human being: 'Is what you are saying a recognition of a truth which really matters to you, something which you have perceived yourself, or are you just testing someone else's allegation?'

This double level of meaning continues right through the dialogue between Jesus and Pilate. Jesus is both the accused and the interrogator; Pilate is both a magistrate and a person under deep scrutiny.

Pilate feels the sting of the question. All the armour he wears as the administrator of imperial law cannot shield him from it. He moves away, for a moment, from the legal role, and takes a stand based upon his cultural and racial status. He relies on the effortless superiority of his privileged Roman identity to protect him. 'I – am *I* a Jew? I'm not bothered about the fiddling preoccupations of you wretched people. It's your own race and your own religious leaders who have brought you here.' He stresses the social and racial distance between himself and Jesus. Having thus reminded Jesus – and himself – that he is boss, he can return to the role where he is confident and competent, that of the role of officer of the law. He asks, 'What have you been doing?'

According to the law, what matters is not what fancy titles a person may give himself, but what actions that person has committed. Jesus, however, does not allow Pilate to have it so easy. He does not directly answer the question of what he has been doing. He knows the key question remains – that of what authority he has been claiming; this will decide whether or not he is guilty of subversion and is therefore a danger to the state. And it will also be the key question to discover whether there is something in Pilate's human make-up which can go deeper than the role of a lawyer, deeper even than the identity of a Roman citizen, to something which can recognize the truth which Jesus represents for him and for every human being.

So Jesus answers by clarifying the meaning of the word 'king', in so far as it applies to him. He does so, however, not in merely theoretical terms but by reference to the behaviour of his followers. This is the evidence for the kind of kingly authority which he represents, and Pilate should be able to see that this could not support a charge of subversion. Jesus has not encouraged his followers to behave as terrorists or soldiers.

We get our picture of the meaning of a word like 'king', 'president' or 'Prime Minister' from what we see of the actual behaviour of kings or presidents or Prime Ministers – or of potential kings or presidents or Prime Ministers. That is how our definitions are formed. The Roman Empire had plenty of experience of different kinds of kings and political leaders. Jesus' explanation ought to be perfectly clear to anyone with Pilate's political training and competence: 'My kingdom is not of this world.' My kingdom does not arise out of the normal conflicts and divisions of society. It is not another power system in competition with the existing power systems. Ultimately, all those systems are systems of unbelief and despair, because they all depend for their survival on competition with and defeat of other groups. If my kingdom were like that, then my followers would behave like the members of any other competitive group; they would use violent and destructive means to secure my survival and to put me on top. But my kingdom works with a different kind of power, a power quite unlike that which is normal in Pilate's Empire.

Jesus is offering Pilate the opportunity to think through the real meaning of power and authority. But Pilate has not got where he is by taking lectures on such matters from voteless, native preachers. For him, all these distinctions are diversions from the main issue. Whatever subtle meaning Jesus may wish to attribute to the word, the fact remains that he seems to call himself a king, and that raises problems which someone in Pilate's position cannot afford to overlook. 'Aha, so you *are* a king, then!'

Jesus sees the need to avoid getting trapped into incriminating himself in the Governor's eyes. Even if he is going to be convicted unjustly, he wants to make sure that this will not be due to a legal mistake, a technical error in the handling of evidence. This is important, if only to safeguard those who are later going to be accused and convicted of being his followers. 'It is you who brought up the word "king",' he says. He does not repudiate the title, but this is not the primary issue of which he wishes to speak, rather: 'My primary concern, my real reason for being here at all, is not a matter of being a king – whatever that may mean – but is in bearing witness to the truth. Anyone who is really open to the truth will recognize my integrity.'

If Pilate will allow himself to recognize who Jesus really is and what he really stands for, he will recognize Jesus' authority; he will recognize in what sense he is a king and in what sense he is not. He will see that Jesus is not a threat to the authority of Pilate or of the State, provided that Pilate and the State are themselves governed by the authority of the truth. But this requires that Pilate should make a judgement concerning Jesus, not just with his legal skill, but with his whole human awareness. Can Pilate come out of the role of lawyer and off his perch of cultural superiority, and meet Jesus genuinely as person to person? Evidently not. He confines himself to the question of subversion; the whole question of truth, in Jesus' sense, is irrelevant to him. 'What is truth?' is Pilate's defence against getting involved in matters which go beyond his professional role.

Pilate refuses to face Christ, who is himself the truth about Pilate, and unless he is willing to face the truth about himself at this deeper level he will find that he is unable to stand up even for conventional justice. He will be defenceless against the power of the corporate lie which is going to bring about the execution of the innocent. His failure to face the deeper question about himself as a person leads directly to his functional failing as a judge.

Jesus shows that he values the traditions and processes of law as a good form of human wisdom for the ordering of society, and the protection of the innocent. The values of the legal profession are affirmed by Jesus. But the question remains: the practitioners of law are trained in the many details of legal procedure and jurisprudence; but are they trained – indeed, can they be trained – in the identifying and recognition of truth?

Pilate is in charge. He can decide that the conversation has gone on long enough. He is not going to be drawn into abstract philosophical questions – that is not his job at this early hour of the morning and with the religious leaders breathing down his neck. As an administrator he is satisfied. He has come to a decision. He goes out to the religious leaders. He goes from the inner question of truth to the outer question of subversion. He announces that there is no case for the accused to answer.

This should be the end of the story. The verdict is very important. For followers of Jesus in later years, it provides helpful guidelines concerning the kind of sympathy and assessment which may be expected from secular law. Officers of the State, in their capacity as officers of the State, cannot be expected to respond to or understand what followers of Jesus have to say about their deepest motives, their commitment to the truth as expressed by Jesus. This kind of truth does not come within the secular State's terms of reference. When Christians try to express their deepest motivations and commitments in a law court, their words will seem to make little sense; they will not fit into the categories of the law.

The same will be true when they try to explain themselves in the self-appointed tribunals organized by the press. The chances are the press will not report that part of the defence which is most important to the defendant.

Pilate has asked the accused to state what he has done. But he knows that the accused is really on trial not for his actions, but for his attitude. However, no one may be legally penalized for holding an attitude, so some other offence must be alleged; for example, the accused may be accused, not of uttering words, but of uttering words in a particular place or context. To the accused, the context may be secondary; the real issue is whether a person is allowed to hold these views or utter these words at all. But the magistrate must judge according to the law; the law will be venturing on to dangerous ground if it investigates beliefs and opinions too far. That road leads to the rule of the 'thought police'; and this is not unknown in nations which have called themselves Christian.

So what can Christian believers hope for if they are brought to trial? We can hope for a verdict that we are not guilty of subversion, and that our actions and beliefs do not endanger the safety of the State or the common good. We should also be able to demonstrate that, if our actions in obedience to Christ are illegal, the fault is with the law and not with us. Unless improper pressures have caused the State to make bad laws, or unless other improper pressures are bending the agents of the law away from their proper impartiality, the Christian may expect to be found not guilty, even though the defence may not be intelligible to the law's officers. Pilate, as magistrate, could see and declare Jesus' innocence, even though, as human being, he could not face Jesus' question concerning the truth.

But the Christian community cannot simply retire into privacy and be satisfied with this negative verdict. It must press the question of truth on to the agents of the law and on to public opinion. It knows that if people are not held by a truth which goes deeper than the truth of the law, they will be vulnerable to the lie – to ideologies, stereotypes, myths, prejudices and all sorts of self-interest, which will lead to false judgement and to injustice; and the justice of the State will not be immune to this infection. Pilate was able to declare Jesus innocent, but he was unable to stand up against the ideological passion which inspired Jesus' accusers. Jesus was crucified under Pontius Pilate.

So the Christian community must continually speak to the government, just as Jesus spoke to Pilate. In the case of a country which claims to have a democratic system, the Church has to address the whole electorate, who are responsible for bringing the government to power, and who, even if they do not vote for it, permit the government to exist and who function as legitimate opposition. The Church has to work for the recognition of truth and falsehood, to expose the convenient 'lies of tongue and pen, the easy speeches that comfort cruel men'. It has to do this 'using words only when necessary', as St Francis counselled his evangelists. It has to live as the fellowship of the Christ who identifies himself with those who get least advantage from the present systems, and who makes new relationships between those who otherwise would have nothing in common. If it fails, it will become – like Caiaphas – merely the religious mouthpiece of a scared, proud, self-centred group. If it is going to ask the Government whether or not it is taking Pilate as a model of good administration, it first has to decide whether its own life is modelled on that of Caiaphas.

An idea occurs to Pilate. Perhaps there is an easy way out. In view of his clear statement, 'I find no case against him', Pilate's duty is to discharge the prisoner straight-away, however unpopular this might be with the local native leadership. But perhaps he can persuade them to accept a compromise. He will not publicly insist on Jesus' innocence: he will give Jesus the benefit of an amnesty. Now, an amnesty makes sense only in the case of someone who is guilty and convicted. Pilate is willing to deprive a genuine candidate of the benefit of the amnesty; he is willing to grant Jesus a favour which logically can be granted only to a guilty person. There-fore, this amounts to a tacit admission that Jesus is guilty.

This tactic fails. The decision concerning Jesus cannot be evaded by tricks of this kind, which only bring further embarrassment. The local people very reasonably demand that, if there is going to be an amnesty for anyone, it should be for someone who really *has* been convicted for offences against the Roman State. Other-wise, Pilate is giving an amnesty on the cheap. Pilate is setting himself up as the administrator of the Sabbath and Jubilee provisions of the law of Moses, which require a regular occasion for the release of debtors. He recognizes this as a Jewish custom – which had its counterpart within Roman tradition also. But there is no point in using this law as a pretext for releasing someone who is not in debt at all. The very fact that the Roman Governor would obviously like the local people to accept Jesus as the candidate for the amnesty this year is enough to put them on their guard. If the Roman Governor is telling us that Jesus is innocent, this shows us that Jesus is not the man for us. Let's take the chance to get a genuine terrorist released. 'Not this man; we want Barabbas.'

Jesus has been arrested like a terrorist, and is innocent. Barabbas is really guilty of terrorism, and is released.

Pilate's own superior and sarcastic style contributes to the failure of his little plan. He is not content to ask the local people if they would accept Jesus of Nazareth in this amnesty; he has to get in a little dig at them by calling him 'King of the Jews'. His sense of humour contributes to the anger of the crowd. By this time, even if Pilate suggested something sensible and just, he would not be heard. He is allowing his own cultural feeling to corrupt his competence as an administrator. He insists on stressing the wide gap between himself and those whom he governs, and this weakens him as a judge. It contributes to the process which crucifies Jesus.

The name 'Barabbas' means 'Son of Father'. It is a universal name. In many cultures, this is the most common way in which surnames are formed. The fact that each of us is the child of our father is undeniably important. Racism says that it is supremely important, that our ancestral identity is the vital quality before which everything else must take second place. For followers of Jesus, a new identity replaces this racial identity. The community which rejected Jesus did so because it felt that Jesus was a threat to its survival and national identity. So it voted for Barabbas. Indeed, everyone in this story, with the exception of Jesus, is driven by the need to secure their own survival at the expense of the survival of someone else – Caiaphas, Pilate, the local community, the disciples; most specifically, this worked for Barabbas. Jesus was the one person for whom survival was not pursued or organized. So he became the first whom God resurrected.

It was not only the secular overlord that crucified Jesus, nor was it the nationalist religious leadership. The death of Jesus was the result of an overwhelming democratic decision. A candidate in a democratic election is always saying outwardly, 'Vote for me'. But in fact the message of the candidate's policy and advertising is designed to say to the voter, 'Vote for yourself'. Those who have the vote, vote. They vote for themselves. They vote for Barabbas. Jesus, at this point, is the one person with no vote. He is the non-citizen. Barabbas wins the election; unanimously.

For Group Work

General Questions

- How does this story fit into my experience?

- What bells does it ring for me?

- Have I ever been in the same situation as one of the characters in the story?

Specific Questions

1 What do you think of Pilate thus far in the story? What impression has he made on you?

2 How far do you think a person of one background can be a judge of someone of another background – for instance, across a big divide of social class or race? Could you invite a judge, magistrate or police officer to go through the story with you, and share with you their own experience of making judgements?

3 In your particular place and time what should your church be saying to government – national government, local authority, town or community council, etc?

4 In the last general election, where do you think Jesus would have fitted in?

For Prayer

Lord Jesus
by your cross and resurrection	**deliver us**
by your witness to the truth	**deliver us**
by your passion and death	**deliver us**
by your victory over the grave	**deliver us**
from the lust for power	**deliver us**
from the conspiracy of silence	**deliver us**
from the worship of weapons	**deliver us**
from the slaughter of the innocent	**deliver us**

from the nightmare of hunger	**deliver us**
from the peace that is no peace	**deliver us**
from security that is no security	**deliver us**
from the politics of terror	**deliver us**
from the plundering of the earth's resources	**deliver us**
from the dispossession of the poor	**deliver us**
from the despair of this age	**deliver us**
by the light of the gospel	**give us peace**
by the good news for the poor	**give us peace**
by your healing of our wounds	**give us peace**
by faith in your word	**give us peace**
by hunger and thirst for justice	**give us peace**
by the coming of your kingdom	**give us peace**

Amen.

O God of truth, whose living word
upholds whate'er hath breath,
look down on thy creation, Lord,
enslaved by sin and death.

Set up thy standard, Lord, that we
who claim a heavenly birth,
may march with thee to smite the lies
that vex thy ransomed earth.

Ah, would we join that blest array,
and follow in the might
of him, the faithful and the true,
in raiment clean and white?

We fight for truth? We fight for God?
Poor slaves of lies and sin!
He who would fight for thee on earth
must first be true within.

Then, God of truth, for whom we long,
thou who wilt hear our prayer,
do thine own battle in our hearts,
and slay the falsehood there.

Yea, come! Then, tried as in the fire,
from every lie set free,
thy perfect truth shall dwell in us,
and we shall live in thee.

T. Hughes (1823–96)
Hymns Ancient and Modern Revised

4

The Person and the Nation

Pilate's Decision

John 19:1–16

Narrator Then Pilate took Jesus and had him whipped. The soldiers made a crown out of thorny branches and put it on his head; then they put a purple robe on him and came to him.

Soldiers Long live the King of the Jews!
1 and 2

Narrator And they went up and slapped him.
Pilate went out once more and said to the crowd:

Pilate Look, I will bring him out here to you to let you see that I cannot find any reason to condemn him.

Narrator So Jesus came out, wearing the crown of

	thorns and the purple robe.
Pilate	Look! Here is the man!
Narrator	When the chief priests and the temple guards saw him, they shouted:
Priest	Crucify him!
Soldiers 1 and 2	Crucify him!
Pilate	You take him, then, and crucify him. I find no reason to condemn him.
Person 1	We have a law that says he ought to die, because he claimed to be the Son of God.
Narrator	When Pilate heard this, he was even more afraid. He went back into the palace [and asked Jesus]:
Pilate	Where do you come from?
Narrator	But Jesus did not answer. (PAUSE)
Pilate	You will not speak to me? Remember, I have the authority to set you free and also to have you crucified.
Jesus	You have authority over me only because it was given to you by God. So the man who handed me over to you is guilty of a worse sin.
Narrator	When Pilate heard this, he tried to find a way to set Jesus free. But the crowd shouted back:
Person 2	If you set him free, that means that you are not the Emperor's friend!
Person 1	Anyone who claims to be a king is a rebel against the Emperor!
Narrator	When Pilate heard these words, he took Jesus outside and sat down on the judge's

seat in the place called 'The Stone Pave-
ment'. In Hebrew the name is 'Gabbatha'.
It was then almost noon of the day before
the Passover. [Pilate said to the people:]

Pilate *(to all)*	Here is your king!
Persons *1 and 2*	Kill him!
Soldiers *1 and 2*	Kill him!
Priest	Crucify him!
Pilate	Do you want me to crucify your king?
Priest	The only king we have is the Emperor!
Narrator	Then Pilate handed Jesus over to them to be crucified.

Pilate has another trick up his sleeve. Perhaps if he pun-
ishes Jesus by torture, and makes him look wretched
and ridiculous, he will satisfy the local community while
still showing who is in charge. But this is merely a further
descent into injustice. There can be no legal justification
for the appalling brutality of scourging. He orders his
soldiers to participate in this criminal procedure. He is
supposed to be the administrator of the somewhat shaky
peace with which the Romans blessed their subject
nations. His soldiers are supposed to be a peacekeeping
force for the benefit of the local community; and certainly the *Pax Romana* worked benignly over a huge
area for a remarkably long time. But even peace keeping
can be a brutalizing task, unless the senior officers take
effective steps to prevent this. Pilate, as commanding

officer, perhaps does more harm to his soldiers than he does to Jesus.

There are only two purposes for such a terrible treatment of another human being. One is to punish so as to deter other offenders. The other is to extract information. Jesus is innocent; punishment is clearly wrong. Is the scourging, therefore, torture for information, a method of extracting the truth? But torture cannot extract truth from one who is already true. Torture cannot make Jesus speak more truthfully than he has already spoken. This whole brutal enterprise is another piece of wasted effort on the part of the powers of the lie and of darkness.

In the absence of any remotely justifiable purpose, we have to conclude that the scourging and mockery are cruelty for its own sake and mockery for its own sake. The soldiers pick up from their commanding officer a frivolous and scornful attitude towards the local community, and particularly towards this prisoner – the whole 'King of the Jews' bit is a joke. This kind of mockery and humour is another way of showing who is in charge. It is a sure way of telling who is 'in' and who is 'out' of the elite circle that can appreciate the joke. The other ranks no doubt have all the usual reasons for disliking the officers; but at this point they are only too willing to make the officers' behaviour their own.

So Jesus is dressed up in make-believe royal regalia, at a time when he is exhausted by the scourging and therefore looking as unkingly as possible. The crowning and obeisance to the 'King of the Jews' is all part of the rubbishing of the subject race, the native community.

But mockery is a dangerous weapon. It may convey exactly the opposite of what is intended. All through the story, the emphasis has been on the authority of Jesus. Now Jesus is given the insignia appropriate to that authority. Made in jest, it states the truth. God takes the cruel humour and cultural self-confidence of this ruling minority, and uses them to proclaim the truth. God, the source of all truth, and the Father of him who is the truth, takes the crookedness of the intended lie and straightens it to state the gospel.

Pilate goes out ahead of Jesus, and warns the crowd that he is bringing him out so that they can see that no further punishment is needed. In spite of the punishment already inflicted, he announces again his verdict that Jesus is innocent.

Jesus comes out, in his tatty regalia, and with bleeding flesh; people can see what a humiliated figure he presents. Pilate makes one of those massive statements which breaks the limitations of its intended meaning. 'Behold the man . . . Look, this is the person concerned.' (The word usually translated as 'man' means 'man' as distinct from 'animal' or 'thing'; it is not 'man' as distinct from 'woman', for which there is a quite different word in Greek. As a human being, you do not have to be male in order to identify with Jesus, in order to be represented by him, or in order to represent him. Jesus is *the* human being.) This is the one whom all the fuss is about – is he worth it? This is the one with the claim to be king – ridiculous! Look, this is the human person – showing what people look like when other people have done their worst with them. Look, this is a person, a real person, complete, proper, genuine: humanity as humanity was designed to be. Look, this is the true human person, the person for you. What are you going to say about him? What are you going to do about him? He stands before you; he demands an answer. The leaders of the most morally educated religious culture in existence cry out, as if possessed by demons, 'Crucify him.'

Pilate is, in principle, on the side of Jesus, because he is, in principle, on the side of justice. He is defending Jesus against an attack which he sees as irrational. But Pilate has been attempting a compromise between the demands of justice and the demands of a powerful lie. Between these he finds that he cannot be impartial. His attempt to placate the religious lie fails; he does not succeed in defusing the hostility to Jesus. On the contrary, like so many detached, uninvolved and superior people, he has miscalculated both the motivations and the depth of feeling in the oppressed community over which he is supposed to rule. They are not thankful for small mercies. It is useless to tell them that they have won a symbolic victory. They have set their hearts on getting rid of Jesus, who seems to them to endanger their national purity and to threaten the economic basis of the temple, and they are not going to let this agent of a foreign imperialism stand in their way. Their irrational demand throws Pilate off his judicial calm. 'All right, you do the crucifying yourselves, then.' If they did so, they would, of course, be breaking the law in a most glaring way; the excuse that they were merely doing what the Governor told them to do would not save them; they would pay for such defiance with their lives – especially as Pilate, yet again, is saying that Jesus has no charges to answer.

This at least has the result of forcing the accusers to make a specific accusation for the first time. Jesus has claimed to be a son of a god. They might well feel that this is a rather weak accusation, and not likely to impress Pilate very much, because it sounds as if all that is wrong with Jesus is that he makes silly religious statements, not that he is politically dangerous. In fact, however, for the first time Pilate is scared – the only point in the whole story where there is a direct comment about anyone's emotions. Why is he scared? Is it because he realizes at last that the accusers are motivated by a profound 'faith commitment', and not just by some stupid spitefulness which might well blow over? Or is it because the rational, superior, secular person cannot live long amidst religious fervour without getting unwittingly infected by it? Is he afraid that there might be something in it after all? Without a commitment to a truth which goes beyond law and science and cultural self-confidence, the secular person is poorly protected against irrational and cruel superstition.

So Pilate goes back to Jesus, to the place where he faces the most difficult questions. He starts with a question of his own: 'Where are you from?' Unknown to Pilate, this is the question which has been raging round Jesus for years. How is it to be answered? From Nazareth? From heaven? From Galilee? From the devil? From the Father? From above? For the accusers of Jesus, it is sufficient to state where he comes from in geographical and social terms, and this is sufficient reason for dismissing his claim to be heard. This is unfaith, for it takes no account of the possibility that people can be anything other than the products of their background. It is an unfaith which is especially attractive to those who rule and to those who aid the rulers by making social classifications, for it asserts the essential predictability of human beings. In the company of faith Jesus has been willing to speak deeply about where he comes from, and the significance of his origins. But in the present context there is nothing to be gained by trying to give a truthful answer to the question, so Jesus is silent.

This silence to an apparently simple question comes across to Pilate as virtual contempt of court, and he brings out the big stick. He reminds this awkward prisoner that he, Pilate, has power to release and power to crucify. Pilate's power to crucify is undeniable. But, as the story goes on to show, he is in process of losing his power to release. He would like to release, but cannot, because he is constrained by forces which go beyond the power of Caesar's representative to control. Jesus, the truth, can set free. Jesus, the truth, could have set Pilate free; but Pilate was not willing to face the question of truth which Jesus put to him. 'So,' says Jesus, 'remember that the power you have is not your own; you are answerable to the higher authority who has delegated it to you.'

This is, on one level, a simple statement of political fact: Pilate is responsible for the proper handling of Caesar's law, and will be answerable for actions which would bring that law into disrepute. Pilate has been given authority in Caesar's interest, not merely so as to be able to get himself out of a personal embarrassment. But even Caesar's law is not merely to serve Caesar's interests, or to ensure the dominance of the powerful. Jesus is insisting that there is a deeper level to Pilate's authority. That authority is fundamentally a blessing, a gift of God. It is not an invention of the devil; nor is it merely an instrument of the will of the ruling class. No, Pilate is answerable to God, and should use his authority as a responsible servant of God. Here, Jesus is speaking as an entirely orthodox inheritor of the Jewish under-standing of the law. The people of Israel had this unique blessing, of being the one people on the face of the earth who could demonstrate that society could indeed be ordered according to the just mind of God – on the basis of a willing sharing of wealth and of knowledge, and with compassion for the poor and the outsider. The secular State cannot be expected to know this inner authority of the law, so the community which con-sciously seeks to follow God's will has to teach and bear witness to it. The religious authorities are supposed to be the specialists in the things of God. It is their duty to remind the State of the source of its authority. So if they fail to do this, and if, on the contrary, they try to persuade the State to use its authority for the per-petration of injustice, their guilt is far higher than that of the State. In the case of Jesus, the official representa-tives of religion are seeking to bend and debase secular justice in order to satisfy the demands of their own self-interest. They are saying to the State: we hear you repeatedly saying that according to the law this man should be set free, but we will not cease to harass you until you treat him as guilty, in order to protect our interests.

Secular justice is a good thing. In normal circumstances it has enough authority to protect itself from pressures which could threaten to divert it from its proper character. Where it is deflected, this is a sign that fears and anxieties and prejudices are making the preservation of justice less important than the preservation of self. Where justice is expendable, Christ is expendable. And Christ will be 'numbered with the transgressors' – identified with those who are counted expendable and not worth valuing. But the primary guilt will lie not with the administrators of justice but with those groups which press the claims of prejudice, and with those groups which fail to warn and to witness to the dangers of false myths and motivations. Caiaphas causes Pilate's fall. Without Caiaphas, Pilate would remain an insensitive, fallible, but basically reliable administrator of a law which still, in spite of its cruelties, commands civilized respect to this day. On the structural level, Pilate has much greater power than Caiaphas; but those who have the greatest power do not necessarily cause the greatest damage.

The Gospel writers, especially John, are sometimes accused of an anti-Jewish bias, and of whitewashing Pilate. Certainly, after Auschwitz and Belsen, we need to acknowledge the ways in which these stories have been employed to justify the most vicious evils of anti-Semitism. But the primary motive of the story is not to tell Gentiles to put the blame on Jews. In the story,

Jesus, Peter, Judas, Annas, Caiaphas and the crowd are all Jews. The primary motive is that the deepest threat to Christ is from those who ought to be able to recognize and follow him, who share his own culture and background. 'He came to his own, and his own received him not.' The key question for the Gospel reader, whether Jew or Gentile, is: if we are 'his own' now, how is he being received, now? Pilate may scare us as an external problem, as the secular judge who does not share our basic ideals. But Caiaphas is the danger from within the religious system itself. As a religious organization, the Church will need to be more vigilant against the Caiaphas within itself, than against the Pilate who may seem to be the more obvious threat from outside.

Jesus states clearly that he recognizes that Pilate has authority. Jesus is no anarchist. He is not a danger to the security of the State. But this is on the understanding that the State itself recognizes that it is not autonomous, that its authority is 'from above'. So Pilate, yet again, seeks to release Jesus. The religious leaders realize that the blasphemy issue is going to get them nowhere, and they return to the specifically political accusation. They formally make the allegation, which Pilate has already in principle disposed of, that Jesus is aiming at usurping political power and therefore is the inevitable enemy of Caesar. Pilate cannot avoid taking judicial notice of such an accusation; if he should fail to do so, his own loyalty to Caesar would be publicly compromised. If Pilate had been grasped by the truth of Jesus at an earlier stage, he would have been able to see through the falsity of this accusation and not be thrown off course by it. But he is not, at a sufficiently deep level, committed to the truth. He has been trying to be impartial between truth and falsehood, and it doesn't work. He submits to the blackmail. But at the same time he realizes that, in making this accusation, the religious leaders are in effect claiming to stand for the interests of Caesar. If Pilate can seize the opportunity, he can get a unique political advantage in his relationship with the nationalist leadership.

For the first time, Pilate takes up the formal role of president of a legal tribunal. The moment of crisis has come, and the Evangelist records it as precisely as possible, as to time and date and place. The name of the place is given in the local religious language and in the cultural language of the Empire. The moment in time is recorded in liturgical, sacrificial time and in universal, clock time.

At this central moment Pilate makes his clearest statement: 'Look, your King'; again, a statement with layer upon layer of meaning. For Pilate, it is untruth full of biting scorn. For the local nationalist leaders, it is untruth full of outrageous insult. For the followers of Jesus, it is the very core and heart of the truth. This Jesus, on his wild way into the darkness to God, is indeed King. He is king of the human religious motive, which can so easily be claimed by the powers of darkness to serve the lie. He is king of the human political motive, which can so easily be manipulated away from the divine mandates of justice and compassion. Those who acknowledge Jesus as king realize that Jesus completely redefines our human ideas of what kingship and authority mean. As followers of Jesus, we do not bend the picture of Jesus so that it will fit our conventional ideas of kingship and authority. From now on we will scrutinize kingship and authority by the test of whether they reflect something of the kingship and authority of Jesus, the crucified one.

The answer to Pilate is the demonic yell, 'Crucify him!' He goads them further: 'Is it your king that I am to crucify?' He gets the answer that he has been angling for, the only logical answer that the religious leaders can make: 'We have no king but Caesar.'

Yes, we demand Roman execution for this man. Our little tribal system is not enough. Our little tribal authority is not enough. We don't have any faith in our traditional government; the eternal God of our fathers is no king for us now. We can say goodbye to everything that we have called our own, to destroy this one man. We have no king but Caesar.

This is the most extraordinary word, spoken by one of the most patriotic and nationalistic people that has ever existed. In the crisis caused by Jesus, they abandon their most cherished and fundamental identity. Like Peter, in denying Jesus they deny themselves. All that has given them identity in the past, all their hopes for a future Messiah-king, all are expendable for the sake of getting rid of this one man. This is Pilate's prize. He extracts from the Jews this acknowledgement of Caesar's authority, going far beyond anything that the State could expect from this proud and independent community. He trades the life of Jesus for this statement of submission to Caesar. For Pilate, a good day's work. As his part of the bargain, he gives the orders which only he can give. Jesus is finally handed over for crucifixion.

As controller of a subject nation, Pilate wins. As the representative of justice and law, Pilate loses. This unbelieving, cynical and sarcastic agent of the best law in the world is ultimately beaten by the scared and devious representatives of the best religion in the world. But he has kept the battle going for six hours. He has gained time for the accused, and this can often be to a defendant's advantage. He thwarts the High Priest's original hope for a quick execution at an early hour without publicity. Seven times he has moved back and forth between the public rostrum and the private interview room. Three times he has formally declared Jesus innocent. This will be of immense importance to the followers of Jesus in due course; any group which makes no secret of the fact that its founder and leader suffered the fate reserved for convicted terrorists must be able to demonstrate that they themselves are not by definition enemies of the State.

Pilate's tragedy is that he has trusted only in the law and has looked for a solution within the limits of the law. His refusal of the invitation to face the claims of a deeper truth about himself has left him vulnerable to manipulation by the forces of untruth. Caesar's representative gives way to the pressure of public opinion, which, even if it has no authority in itself, and even if it is the voice of a voteless and oppressed people, is able to twist the wills of those who hold authority. Pilate finds himself trapped into being an accomplice in the death of the Son of God.

For Group Work

General Questions

- How does this story fit into my experience?

- What bells does it ring for me?

- Have I ever been in the same situation as one of the characters in the story?

Specific Questions

1 Who do you see as the authority figures in your world – both locally and in the wider world? How far do you see them as reflecting God's authority?

2 Could you invite a Jewish person to read the story with you and to share their impressions? What are we Christians missing because of our poor relationship with Jews? What have we to learn from them?

3 Have you suffered because of someone else's attempts at humour or sarcasm – particularly someone more powerful than yourself? What did it feel like? Do you recall occasions when you have tried to be humorous at someone else's expense, or when

someone else was being made to look ridiculous?
What was really going on?

4 When is the time to be silent?

For Prayer

I walked through the lonely streets,
And I sat with the faceless ones,
And made friends with forgotten folk,
But you never saw me.
>   **O Lord, O what have we done,**
>   **for we never find you among us?**

I stood close to your window pane,
And I knocked on your tight-shut door;
But so full and busy is life,
Who am I to disturb you?
>   **O Lord, O what have we done,**
>   **for we never find you among us?**

I gave you a hammer and nails
And wood from a living tree:
And, just for the carpenter's son,
What a present you made for me.
>   **O Lord, O what have we done,**
>   **for we never find you among us?**

To those whose eyes were blind,
I gave light so that they could see;
But what can I do for you
Whose look is seldom for me?
> **O Lord, O what have we done,**
> **for we never find you among us?**

'Contemporary Reproaches', from *Wild Goose
Songs, Vol. 2*, the Iona Community

Here hangs a man discarded,
a scarecrow hoisted high,
a nonsense pointing nowhere
to all who hurry by.

Can such a clown of sorrows
still bring a useful word
where faith and love seem phantoms
and every hope absurd?

Can he give help or comfort
to lives to comfort bound,
when drums of dazzling progress
give strangely hollow sound?

Life emptied of all meaning,
drained out in deep distress,

can share in broken silence
my deepest emptiness.

And love that freely entered
the pit of life's despair
can name our hidden darkness
and suffer with us there.

Lord, if you now are risen,
help all who long for light
to hold the hand of promise
and walk into the night.

From Brian Wren, *Mainly Hymns*

5

Finishing the Work

Jesus is crucified

John 19:17–37

Narrator   Jesus went out, carrying his cross, and came to 'The Place of the Skull', as it is called. In Hebrew it is called 'Golgotha'. There they crucified him; and they also crucified two other men, one on each side, with Jesus between them. Pilate wrote a notice and had it put on the cross.

Pilate   Jesus of Nazareth, the King of the Jews.

Narrator   Many people read it, because the place where Jesus was crucified was not far from the city. The notice was written in Hebrew, Latin, and Greek. The chief priests said to Pilate:

Priest   Do not write 'The King of the Jews', but

rather, 'This man said, I am the King of the Jews.'

Pilate   What I have written stays written.

Narrator   After the soldiers had crucified Jesus, they took his clothes and divided them into four parts, one part for each soldier. They also took the robe, which was made of one piece of woven cloth without any seams in it. [The soldiers said to one another:]

Soldier 1
(to
Soldier 2)   Let's not tear it.

Soldier 2
(to
Soldier 1)   Let's throw dice to see who will get it.

Narrator   This happened in order to make the scripture come true:

Psalmist   They divided my clothes among themselves and gambled for my robe.

Narrator   And this is what the soldiers did. (PAUSE) Standing close to Jesus' cross were his mother, his mother's sister, Mary the wife of Clopas, and Mary Magdalene. Jesus saw his mother and the disciple he loved standing there; so he said to his mother:

Jesus   He is your son.

Narrator   Then he said to the disciple:

Jesus   She is your mother.

Narrator   From that time the disciple took her to live in his home. (PAUSE)

             Jesus knew that by now everything had

	been completed; and in order to make the scripture come true, he said:
Jesus	I am thirsty.
Narrator	A bowl was there, full of cheap wine; so a sponge was soaked in the wine, put on a stalk of hyssop, and lifted up to his lips. Jesus drank the wine and said:
Jesus	It is finished! (PAUSE)
Narrator	Then he bowed his head and died.
	The Jewish authorities asked Pilate to allow them to break the legs of the men who had been crucified, and to take the bodies down from the crosses. They requested this because it was Friday, and they did not want the bodies to stay on the crosses on the Sabbath, since the coming Sabbath was especially holy. So the soldiers went and broke the legs of the first man and then of the other man who had been crucified with Jesus. But when they came to Jesus, they saw that he was already dead, so they did not break his legs. One of the soldiers, however, plunged his spear into Jesus' side, and at once blood and water poured out.
Witness	The one who saw this happen has spoken of it, so that you also may believe. What he said is true, and he knows that he speaks the truth.
Narrator	This was done to make the scripture come true:
Scripture	Not one of his bones will be broken.

Narrator And there is another scripture that says:
Scripture People will look at him whom they pierced.

They take Jesus. Again, the 'they' is an unnamed group, whose function is simply to shift the prisoner around.

Earlier in this Gospel, we are told that the Word of God came to his own, but his own people did not receive him (exactly the same word). Now he is received, but only as the final sign of his people's refusal of him. From now on, Jesus' 'own people' are no longer to be identified by race, ancestry or religious background. His own people are those who share his commitment and follow him, in continuing to present his crisis to the world.

Jesus is alone. Only he can carry the cross. His obedience means that he can, at the time of crisis, be entirely alone. He goes out to a conspicuous high point outside the city, the place called Cranium, the Skull, the place where legend stated that Adam's skull was buried. Here is the new Adam, the Adam who is the truly human being, fully obedient to the Creator. His death is for all the children of Adam, so it takes place with maximum publicity.

There they crucify him. The Evangelist has gone into great detail about the process leading to this act, and will fill the story out with more detail later. But the act of crucifixion is accounted for in one verb in a subordinate clause. This is all we are told. Crucifixions were common enough; they could conveniently take place three at a time. The Evangelist's readers would know quite enough about the procedure without being reminded of the wretched details. The cross was a ghastly symbol of horror and despair, and did not become an emblem of holiness until a Christian emperor abolished this kind of death penalty. For us, who are not so familiar with the process, perhaps the main thing we need to remember is that crucifixion was not only a terrible form of dying, it was also a terrible way of living. Unlike hanging, electrocution or the firing squad, its purpose was not just to kill, but to display the prisoner alive in an extended period of helplessness. Death normally came not because of wounds, but through exposure and exhaustion. The victim was fixed, almost immobilized, a feast for flies and a target for every feeble person who would take delight in seeing and attacking someone who was powerless. Everyone who is a helpless victim of human rejection, be it criminal or social or individual, is identified with the experience of Jesus. Those who tolerate a society which keeps an underclass with no effective rights or voice, are identifying themselves with the crucifiers of Jesus, even if they are sometimes charitable and caring individuals. The Church has to decide where it finds itself – as an associate of the crucified or of the crucifiers.

Pilate is still angry and full of scorn. He writes the statement of the identity and the crime of the prisoner, 'Jesus of Nazareth, King of the Jews'. The religious leaders have forced him into responsibility for Jesus' execution; let them now have the embarrassment of having to explain away the implications of the publicly displayed charge-sheet. This announcement of

Jesus' identity and crime is being given maximum publicity. Many ordinary people from the city see it. It is
displayed in all the recognized languages of the area, so
that all the peoples of the area – indeed, all the peoples
of the world – can read it. It is written in Hebrew,
the language of religion, the language of the tradition
represented by both Caiaphas and Jesus; in Latin, the
language of the Empire, of the law, the language of the
tradition represented by Pilate; in Greek, the language
of culture, the language of the Evangelist and of the
growing communities addressed by the Evangelist.
There is one message for all groups and all languages.
But each group can find the truth within its own
language, and this Christ is the same Christ as the
Christ who is found within other languages. On the
Day of Pentecost, the Holy Spirit uses and affirms
the validity of the language of 'every nation under
heaven'. Every language and every culture can be the
vehicle for the witness of truth; those who speak the
less powerful languages do not have to become ventrilo-
quist's dummies on behalf of the languages of the powerful. But to every language-group the critical question
comes: can you recognize the crucified one as king for
you?

So the difference of language ceases to be a barrier.
If the Jews, as a group, have a king, this king has to be
shared with the Greeks and the Latins. The proclamation of 'the King of the Jews' in this trilingual form
makes obsolete the vision of a leader who would be
king for the Jews only, or for any one group only. We
are warned against assuming that our own ways of

thinking and speaking are automatically and authentically Christian and therefore superior to those of everyone else. Christ is for all. The expression of his truth is not confined to any single language-group, not even to the language of the group which calls itself Christian. Those who are 'converted' to Christ do not have to change their culture and belong to someone else's. But they do have to acknowledge something which is already true and has always been true, that Christ is king within all our cultures, recognized or unrecognized. He is the consecrator and the most searching critic of every culture; and the crisis is in the fact of a king who is crucified.

Meanwhile, the majority of Christians are Gentile; and we need to remember that the first proclamation of our Christ is that he is King of the Jews. We will not be complete in our recognition of this king until we are led into greater solidarity with those who are still awaiting the Messiah and who believe that he is not yet found. Christ has come, so we say, as king and judge, consecrator and critic, of the tradition which gave him birth. If we hope that the community of Judaism will eventually recognize the truth in Pilate's inscription, firstly we have to acknowledge that Christians have for centuries been treating Jews as Jews treated Jesus, and that Jews therefore have (if they can recognize it) an advantage in recognizing the central symbolisms of the truth that is in Jesus; and secondly we need to rediscover and reaffirm that essential witness to God's sovereignty over society, wealth, the land and the whole creation, represented by the laws of Sabbath and Jubilee, which shaped the kingly authority which Jesus claimed. With-

out the witness of the Jews, we simply do not know
what kind of king Jesus is.

But literacy is not everything. Many people read and
are offended. The truth is dangerous; it can lead to
awkward questions. Freedom of information is not a
principle which appeals to the religious authorities. They
attempt a form of censorship – not to ban statements
which are untrue but to ban statements which are incon-
venient. They do not believe the true statement 'the King
of the Jews'; they ask that it should be replaced by a
strictly untrue statement which they do believe, namely,
'This man said, "I am King of the Jews."' Pilate will
stand no more nonsense from these people. Even though
he does not appreciate the truth of what he has written,
he has committed himself to writing. He is the unrepent-
ant author of this first written Gospel. He has publicly
identified himself with these words and he is not willing
to retract them. A witness to Jesus – even such a compromised witness as Pilate – ultimately does not say, 'This
is what Jesus said about himself', but 'This is what I
say about Jesus.' What we offer is not an academically
correct statement from the past but a statement of our
own understanding and commitment.

There are some occupational perequisites which go
with the job of being a soldier in a colonial force. The
soldiers claim possession of the property of the executed
person. There are four men; they each take a share of
Jesus' clothing: 'This is for me'; 'That's mine.' But only
the external garments can be divided like this. There is
an inner garment, single and seamless. To make a seamless garment is skilled and sophisticated work. Most

garments, whether inner or outer, are made with seams. But there is one person in the local religious tradition for whom a specially made seamless garment is part of the uniform, namely, the High Priest. Jesus has this uniform: he is the true priest, in contrast to Caiaphas; he is the true judge, in contrast to Pilate. In Christ is seen the necessary character of priesthood; the only priest who can offer sacrifice for the needs and pains of the world is the priest who is also victim. The true followers of Jesus form a priestly community, representing the atoning and sacrificial purpose of Jesus. But, to be so, they must have this seamlessness in themselves.

The outer garments can be divided up among four people; the only way to divide the inner garment would be to destroy it. Provided that we are satisfied with the externals, we can parcel out the tradition of Christianity in little bits; we can think of a specially protestant emphasis or a particularly English morality or a uniquely Asian spirituality or even a white Christian civilization. But as long as we do this we show that we are missing the essential heart of the faith: that the real inner truth of Christ is either a unity or it is nothing at all.

If a particular group tries to take Christianity as its own badge, to distinguish itself from others, all it can take is one bit of Jesus' clothing, one external garment. Part of itself will have a Christian identity, and part will be something else; it can have the shirt of Christ and the trousers of middle-class capitalism; or the socks of Jesus and the headgear of anarchist revolution. One fragment of the vesture of Jesus will not be enough to keep out the cold. When the clothes of Jesus are divided, one party will proudly claim to have his boots and another will make a point of possessing his overcoat. They will fail to understand or recognize each other, and they will treat each other as rivals.

To the onlooker, the whole performance will look ridiculous; the Christian movement will be part of the world's problem rather than a hope for its healing. But, beyond all this absurdity, beyond the in-fighting, which gives us such a bad press, there is the inner garment without seams. It cannot be used except as a single garment. It cannot be broken down into its component parts or divided at the joins. It is either all or nothing. Those who, for most of the time, are concerned with their own bit of the outer clothing, can also recognize the truth of this inner garment; and they can recognize it in each other, even if the externals look so different. Just as there is a double meaning when the authority of Pilate is said to be 'from above', so there may be at the point where the inner garment is said to be 'woven from above'. Physically, the garment is fabricated from the neck down; and the communion of Christ's followers is the creation of God, a gift 'from above', not a piece of human organization which can be disposed of according to the wit of administrators. The inner garment is for the Church which is truly integrated, the Church which allows no other tradition or interest to take priority over its commitment to the figure of Jesus Christ. It is the clothing of the 'new Adam' in the midst of the divisions of the old world. The disintegrated Church may appeal to the sectional interest of one group against another.

It will represent a spirituality of opposition, justifying itself by the vigour and precision of its disapproval of other groups. This will attract temporarily. But in a time of crisis it is likely to conceal or discard even that one bit of Christ's clothing, which it has been displaying, and it will stand exposed as a fraud. A spirituality of opposition cannot for long sustain and nourish the human spirit.

So, the soldiers can divide up the outer garments. For the inner garment some other way has to be found of allocating possession. They organize a lottery. They make 'chance' the arbiter of their fortunes. But even as they give fate its authority, they are unwittingly recognizing the authority of the mind of God; for this, according to the Evangelist, is happening in fulfilment of Scripture. God, whose good creative purpose appears to be denied by these terrible events, is still in authority. The small acts of the unbelievers are knit into the fabric of salvation. The mind of God is still at work, even when these people believe that everything is being determined by mindless and purposeless forces.

So there are these four men, sorting out matters of their personal interest during their working hours. In contrast to them there are four women, watching the man die. They have waited and stood around. At this stage the men in the story are either busy with their duties or buried in despair. The women are simply present. All that they can do is to ensure that the man does not die totally alone. Women seem always to have seen the point of doing this. Their presence is not a threat to the authorities. They have the courage and the patience just to be there, alongside. Men can ask themselves why the only men on the scene are the soldiers.

But this is not quite fair. There is one man with the women. There is the man called 'the disciple whom Jesus loved'. He is not called the disciple who loved Jesus. What is important is not his own ability to love, but the fact of his being loved. His lovedness is the one reliable and secure thing about him. He is secure enough to be present authentically in the place of extreme insecurity. Most of us show, for much of the time, that we have not been fully loved; so we are anxious, defensive, paranoid and short of courage. We expect other people to be the same, and plan accordingly. This disciple knows that he is loved; the disciple-church knows that it is loved, and that nothing can separate us from the love of God in Christ. The disciple who is loved can be entrusted with a task of love.

One of the women present is the mother of Jesus. Jesus addresses her, as he has done at significant moments in the past, not as 'Mother' but as 'woman' – an untranslatable term of respect and affection. Although Jesus' cultural group put great value on physical parenthood, Jesus' witness is that this ancestral identity is no longer the most important thing about us. He says to his mother, 'Look, this is your son.' To the disciple he says, 'Look, this is your mother.' Even when he is fixed to the cross, Jesus is still the Creator. He is making new relationships. We take our identity not from our birth, but from the action of Christ in giving us to each other. For the follower of Jesus, the brother or sister or parent or child is not the relative given to us by family or ancestry, but the member of the new family given to us in Christ. Within that family, we say that we are in communion with each other. This communion is not according to any decision or selection of our own; it is the gift of Christ. Within the family, we are given to each other and we accept each other. St Paul uses the helpful image of the adoptive family; within an adoptive family we belong to each other as people who come together out of many different natural families by the choice of the parent. Christ's most precious gift to us is the gift of the new sister or brother. It is not enough to fight for someone else's political rights, or to organize help for them – important though these may be. Christ's gift is that we actually *are* sisters and brothers of each other; any service which we may give to each other starts from that gift. Christ is not laying down a new moral code; he is stating a new personal fact. The disciple whom Jesus loves does not need any instructions, but acts in accordance with the new fact; he takes his new mother home.

This may all seem to be rather domestic and unimportant. In fact, it is the climax of Jesus' whole work and ministry. He has brought into existence the new community, the community which depends on his gift of each of us to the other. People may or may not find the moral teaching of Jesus impressive; they may or may not feel inspired by the Church's worship; they may or may not find that Christian doctrine makes new sense in an unintelligible world. But the real test of discipleship comes at this more basic level, of whether or not we are prepared to take seriously the new community which

Jesus is making. It is in this that the glory and the shame of the Church is to be measured. This was the unprecedented distinguishing mark of the followers of Jesus in the early days of our movement. It was notorious for being responsibly careless about people's qualifications in terms of background, ancestry and religious goodness. This is what attracted people into it. This is what drew upon it the suspicions and hostility of the inheritors of the roles of Caiaphas and Pilate.

When Christ has made this new creation, he has done all that has to be done. All is now finished; it remains only to announce this fact as clearly as possible. There is one vital word to say. Jesus needs a fresh voice to say it with. Even in this detail of his thirst, Scripture is being fulfilled, the mind of God is being worked out in history. Is the offering of sour wine an act of kindness or of cruelty? We cannot tell, and it does not much matter. Jesus is in command; he is able to use his voice just for one moment, one word. He announces to the world that the task is complete. He has done what he came to do. There is no need to linger. '*Tetelestai*! – It is finished!' He rests his head, and stops living.

Jesus does not just die. He does not have his life taken away from him; he is the master, even at this point. He gives his life; he hands over his Spirit. Up to this point the Spirit of Jesus has been his alone, and he alone has been able to do the works of the Spirit. But now he has just created his new community. Now there is the beginning of the new body of Christ, the body which will be given energy and power and meaning by the

Spirit of Jesus living and breathing within it. The very last moment of the life of Jesus is as purposeful as all the moments that have preceded it.

The soldiers are surprised to find that Jesus has died so soon. Most crucified people linger on half dead for hours or even days. This is because there is in us such a resistance to death, such a valuing of life, even when pain would make death welcome. But Jesus is not ruled by the urge for survival. When the crisis which he has brought makes his death a necessary part of the life-sharing purpose, he gives himself to death and does not hang on to life. The whole story of the arrest, trials and crucifixion of Jesus shows that he has found a third way, an alternative to destructive violence on the one hand and passive acquiescence on the other. In his death, also, Jesus finds an alternative to selfish and clinging survival on the one hand, and despairing, fruitless suicide on the other. Even in his dying Jesus is in command and takes the initiative.

The religious authorities have another problem to worry their tender consciences. It would not be proper for the bodies of criminals to be on public display during the annual festival of their Covenant with God. Fundamental injustice may be a regrettable necessity on occasion; but public obscenity is not to be tolerated. The sight of three totally naked dead bodies would be a sign that Caiaphas and his colleagues have lost control of public decency, and that secular carelessness has taken over. So they ask Pilate to hurry up the process of death by having the legs of the crucified men broken. When a crucified man's legs are broken, he cannot stiffen his body to breathe, and he dies of asphyxiation. But Jesus has already handed over his breath (or Spirit); it does not need to be taken from him by violence. So the soldiers find that he is already dead; but they make sure of this by stabbing him in the side with a spear. The Evangelist again sees the significance of the fulfilment of Scripture in these details; the initiatives are still with God, and God is not served by the uncertainties of possible coma or deception.

Pilate could, of course, refuse the request for the bodies to be taken down. Normally, the exposure of the dead body of the crucified is an important part of the whole process; it hangs there indefinitely as a sign of the ruthless power of the Empire and as a deterrent to would-be disturbers of the peace. But deterrence is not so relevant in the case of Jesus. Pilate knows very well that Jesus is no ordinary terrorist; what has happened to Jesus is not going to deter someone who wants to take up weapons of violence against the State. The followers of Jesus believe that the work of Jesus is unique and unrepeatable; deterrence is not relevant to them. Indeed, to the followers of Jesus his crucifixion is not a deterrent, but an invitation to discipleship. And Pilate does not need the rotting body on the cross in order to provide publicity; the publicity is already organized on a far more widespread basis for the information of the whole world. We do not have to make a journey of thousands of miles to see the body of Jesus; Christian faith and commitment are not limited to those who have the privilege of being able to travel to Jerusalem. The meaning of Christ is there to be found in the person next to you, wherever you are. If you do not see it there, it is not going to do the slightest good for you to travel to see the place where he died.

Religion and State make the mistake which inevitably results from unbelief: they do not reckon with the power of God to raise the dead. They assume that because they have got the dead body of Jesus the movement of Jesus is dead also. They do not realize that the death is the cue for a new beginning. They think that now the death has happened, they can get on with their religious and administrative routines without further embarrassment or interference.

But signs of a new beginning can already be seen. In the Evangelist's understanding the flow of blood and water from the wound in Jesus' side is more than just a physical event. Water and blood are life-giving, life-representing substances. Christ is giving his Spirit to his community, and the Spirit works characteristically through these symbols, in the sacraments of baptism and eucharist. Here is the birth of the new body of Christ; the flow of water and blood from the side of Christ never ceases. The crucifixions suffered by members of Christ's body are not isolated tragedies – they are the means by which we share in the programme of salvation once completely fulfilled by our representative, the new Adam. The symbols of water and blood make us sharers in the dying and rising of Christ on behalf of the whole disorder of humankind, the sin of the world.

For Group Work

General Questions

- How does this story fit into my experience?

- What bells does it ring for me?

- Have I ever been in the same situation as one of
  the characters in the story?

Specific Questions

1 Who is being crucified today? Who is being treated
as rubbish, expendable or redundant? Where is the
Church in relationship to them? Where do you think
Christ is in relationship to them? (Try to think both
locally and more widely.)

2 What do your local churches look like to people
living around them? Are there some things which
they have deeply in common, in spite of their
dividedness? How can this essential unity be
affirmed?

3 Is your church evidence of God's power to make a
new family, across all the divisions of the world?
What have you learned from people of a language
or culture different from your own?

For Prayer

Behold the holy Lamb of God
**Behold the one who bears for us a heavy
load;**
Holy Lamb of God
**Lo, upon the cross he bears earth's
sorrows, sin and loss.**
In humble silence, thus goes he,
**In sad procession, Christ the captive
hauls the tree**
Holy Lamb of God
**Lo, upon the cross he bears earth's
sorrows, sin and loss.**
And look, outside the city wall,
**a rubbish dump is where he dies to save
us all**
Holy Lamb of God
**Lo, upon the cross he bears earth's
sorrows, sin and loss.**
What cruel yet blessed agony!
Confronting sin and death, he sets us free.
Holy Lamb of God
**Lo, upon the cross he bears earth's
sorrows, sin and loss.**

Song from Malawi, from *Cloth for the Cradle*,
Iona Community

Lord Christ,
by your cross you have broken down the middle
    wall of partition
that has separated your people from each other;
by the power of your Spirit
reconcile us and all people to God our Father,
and to our sisters and brothers of every age and
    culture,
so that we may no longer be strangers and aliens
    to each other,
but fellow-citizens in the community of saints
in the household of God our Father.
Amen.

6

Burial and Beyond

The empty tomb

John 19:38–20:29

Narrator   After this, Joseph, who was from the town
of Arimathea, asked Pilate if he could take
Jesus' body.

Witness   Joseph was a follower of Jesus, but in
secret, because he was afraid of the Jewish
authorities.

Narrator   Pilate told him he could have the body, so
Joseph went and took it away. Nicodemus,
who at first had gone to see Jesus at night,
went with Joseph, taking with him about
thirty kilogrammes of spices, a mixture of
myrrh and aloes. The two men took Jesus'
body and wrapped it in linen with the
spices according to the Jewish custom of

preparing a body for burial. There was a garden in the place where Jesus had been put to death, and in it there was a new tomb where no one had ever been buried. Since it was the day before the Sabbath and because the tomb was close by, they placed Jesus' body there.

Narrator   Early on Sunday morning, while it was still dark, Mary Magdalene went to the tomb and saw that the stone had been taken away from the entrance. She went running to Simon Peter and the other disciple, whom Jesus loved.

Mary   They have taken the Lord from the tomb, and we don't know where they have put him!

Narrator   Then Peter and the other disciple went to the tomb. The two of them were running, but the other disciple ran faster than Peter and reached the tomb first. He bent over and saw the linen wrappings, but he did not go in. Behind him came Simon Peter, and he went straight into the tomb. He saw the linen wrappings lying there and the cloth which had been round Jesus' head. It was not lying with the linen wrappings but was rolled up by itself. Then the other disciple, who had reached the tomb first, also went in; he saw and believed. They still did not understand the scripture which said that he must rise from death. Then the disciples went back home. (PAUSE)

Mary stood crying outside the tomb. While

she was still crying, she bent over and looked in the tomb and saw two angels there dressed in white, sitting where the body of Jesus had been, one at the head and the other at the feet. [They asked her:]

Angel(s)   Woman, why are you crying?

Mary   They have taken my Lord away, and I do not know where they have put him!

Narrator   Then she turned round and saw Jesus standing there; but she did not know that it was Jesus.

Jesus   Woman, why are you crying? Who is it that you are looking for?

Narrator   She thought he was the gardener.

Mary   If you took him away, sir, tell me where you have put him, and I will go and get him.

Jesus   Mary!

Mary   Rabboni! Teacher!

Jesus   Do not hold on to me, because I have not yet gone back up to the Father. But go to my brothers and tell them that I am returning to him who is my Father and their Father, my God and their God.

Narrator   So Mary Magdalene went and told the disciples that she had seen the Lord and related to them what he had told her.

It was late that Sunday evening, and the disciples were gathered together behind locked doors, because they were afraid of the Jewish authorities. Then Jesus came and stood among them. [He said:]

Jesus   Peace be with you.

Narrator	After saying this, he showed them his hands and his side. The disciples were filled with joy at seeing the Lord. [Jesus said to them again:]
Jesus	Peace be with you. As the Father sent me, so I send you.
Narrator	Then he breathed on them [and said]:
Jesus	Receive the Holy Spirit. If you forgive people's sins, they are forgiven; if you do not forgive them, they are not forgiven.
Narrator	One of the twelve disciples, Thomas (called the Twin), was not with them when Jesus came. So the other disciples told him:
Disciple(s)	We have seen the Lord!
Narrator	Thomas said to them:
Thomas	Unless I see the scars of the nails in his hands and put my finger on those scars and my hand in his side, I will not believe.
Narrator	A week later the disciples were together again indoors, and Thomas was with them. The doors were locked, but Jesus came and stood among them [and said]:
Jesus	Peace be with you.
Narrator	Then he said to Thomas:
Jesus (to Thomas)	Put your finger here, and look at my hands; then stretch out your hand and put it in my side. Stop your doubting, and believe!
Thomas	My Lord and My God!
Jesus	Do you believe because you see me? How happy are those who believe without seeing me!

Crisis does strange things to people. Some well-known people may conveniently be absent; others, who have never come much into the open, may suddenly discover new and surprising courage. It is not Peter and Andrew, but Joseph and Nicodemus who come forward and risk ridicule and disapproval by asking for the corpse of Jesus. They stand up to be counted, although they both have a lot to lose – Nicodemus especially, as a member of the Jewish Council. He previously came to Jesus secretly, under cover of darkness, an interested but fearful seeker after truth. As a councillor, he has tried to speak up for the truth, and has been rudely rebuffed. Now it is dusk; the land is in half-light, and quickly getting darker. The Sabbath is about to begin.

For these two the Sabbath was not primarily the great celebration of joy and release and freedom which it was in the law of Moses, and which it still is today for many grateful Jews. It had become a negative sign, a restriction; for Jesus, the Sabbath has been an obstacle to a ministry of healing and revelation; it has been a convenient tool for his opponents. Now, at this point in the story, this negative side of the Sabbath is having its last fling. It is causing extra hurry and anxiety in an act of kindness and of traditional respect for the dead. These men act with courage and generosity and great energy. But, unintentionally, they are acting as allies of Pilate and Caiaphas; their whole object is to finalize and certify the deadness of Jesus. Jesus is dead; the best we can do is to preserve. But we shall see that preservatives are useless in the presence of the living God. There is no clearer instance of sheer and ineffective waste in the whole history of the world than the massive load of spices with which these good and generous men seek to weigh down the corpse of Jesus and trap it in a hole in the ground. When good and generous friends of Jesus, in our own day, put their honest energies into preserving their Christian inheritance, they find themselves along-side Joseph and Nicodemus. They may be doing their best; but their efforts are doomed.

This is the end of the story of the crisis presented by Christ. In being judged, he has himself been judging the world. He has exposed the untruth of the norms of justice and righteousness that are customary in the world as it is. But even this is not the primary purpose. The Son of God does not come into the world merely to tell us how bad we are. His revelation is not an expression of hatred; it is not intended to reinforce our own hatred, whether of other people or of ourselves. The purpose of Christ is summarized earlier in the Gospel: 'Now is the judgement of this world, now shall the ruler of this world be cast out; and I, when I am lifted up from the earth, will draw all people to myself.' Much indeed, that cannot stand in the face of the crisis Jesus brings, has to be cast out. But the central purpose of this is to clear the way for the new community which is released by Christ and which draws all people into one humanity.

This is what the last part of the Gospel story is about. It is not the end. Easter is not the end, for Easter is still going on; it is where we are now. Easter is how we know about the cross and all that led up to the cross. When the Church is under stress from the world, or when a follower of Jesus is being penalized for faithfulness to Christ, it is easy to see and claim the meaning of the cross. The resurrection may seem very distant. But only through the resurrection can we know Jesus as the crucified one whose crucifixion can have meaning for us. From the teaching of Easter we shall not necessarily come to know many things which are not already there in the story of the crucifixion. But we shall know how the truth of the crucifixion is known, and how it can be living truth for us where we are.

The method and manner of the crucifixion were public for all to see; the method and manner of the resurrection were hidden. No one saw it happen; only the effects become known, and they register with different people in different ways. Gradually the knowledge of it spreads from person to person, and they wake up to the fact that, like Rip van Winkle, they have been 'sleeping through a revolution'. The central witness in the story is Mary Magdalene, and the truth becomes known to her only through a lengthy process, which to a considerable extent, she resists. As we follow the developing awareness of Mary and of Thomas and of the other disciples, we see not only the reactions of individual persons but also models or specimens of how communities and churches respond to the opening up of truth which brings hope and healing.

Mary Magdalene comes to the tomb in the dark. The tragedy of what has happened to Jesus fills her mind; she cannot allow anything else to claim her. Her only security is the certainty that this terrible thing has happened to the one she has loved so deeply. She is so preoccupied by the loss that she interprets everything in terms of the loss; everything that happens serves to strengthen that sense of dereliction. This first experience of the Easter event plunges her even more deeply into a sense of absence. She does not even have a corpse to cherish. As if it were not enough that the Lord has been crucified by the Roman power, now she believes that his body has been vandalized by grave-robbers, presumably attracted by the kingly quantities of spices brought by Nicodemus and Joseph.

Mary must communicate. She cannot keep anything to herself. She does not wait or explore or seek alternative explanations. She immediately runs to tell Peter and the other disciple.

The two men arrive. Peter is the one who notices all the circumstances, the organization of things. He observes the interesting details of the arrangement of the linen cloths, the general orderliness of the scene, as if a person had woken up early in the morning and had tidily made the bed before leaving for work. This is all very fascinating; but the more significant matter is not the things that are there, but the person who is not there. The Evangelist uses two quite distinct words which are both translated into English as 'see': Peter 'sees' as a spectator; the other disciple 'sees' with understanding and commitment. He sees the definite absence of Jesus, and he believes. The living is not to be found in the place of the dead. There is one place on the face of the earth where we are confident that the dead Jesus is to be found, and he is not there. The preservatives have been a waste.

The men do not tell Mary. She is left to her undiluted

grief. She sees angels (messengers) – she sees as a spectator. But this vision does nothing to shake her dedi-
cation to tragedy and mourning. When she sees Jesus
actually present, she assumes that this is the person who
must be responsible for Jesus' absence. For a time Jesus
lets her despair deepen. He lets her pour out the compul-
sive programme of action which she wants to follow. It
is only when he addresses her directly by name, recognizing her for whom she uniquely is, that her preoccupation
with her own feelings is broken. She realizes that she
can be claimed by an interest outside herself, that the
reality of Jesus can replace her own intense feelings
as the centre of her being. For Mary, there have to be
these stages in realization; until she has seen (as a
spectator) without recognizing, she cannot see the truth
(with understanding). She has constructed a picture of
herself which depends on the tragedy and on her own
schemes for fitting herself into the tragedy. The risen
Jesus comes as a fundamental disturbance to that picture
of herself.

It is to Mary Magdalene that the Easter truth first
comes as a personal encounter. She is the first person
to become an apostle of the resurrection, a communi-
cator of the truth. She is scarcely the most obvious kind
of person to choose for such a responsibility. Quite apart
from her distraught and confused state, she is of the
wrong sex for her testimony to be acceptable in a court
of law. But she is the first witness on whom our faith
depends. The disciple-community has to come to terms
with the fact that it is to Mary that we owe our first
knowledge of the great new state of the world which

God has brought about. Her kind of evidence is essential to our movement.

The spiritually strong can, like the beloved disciple, simply see and believe. But this disciple, although he believes immediately and without complication, feels no need to communicate the truth to anyone else. He and Peter merely go home (literally, they go into themselves). If the message came only through the spiritual high-fliers, it might be a splendid and impressive message; but the delivering of it would represent no change to the power systems of the world. If the Son of God had started off his mission by collecting a bunch of articulate graduates from the rabbinic school in Jerusalem and had sent them off to Galilee with some such message as, 'Hey, you peasants, here is some good news for you from headquarters', the world might have been impressed, but there would have been no disturbance of the conventions of the day and the existing lines of power. The character-istic manner of Gospel communication is that it starts with people on the edge and moves towards people at the centre. Mary speaks first. The others will get their chance.

Mary needs a task, an active outlet. Jesus gives her the mission of communicating with the disciple-community. Furthermore, she has to realize that, just as the old situ-ation of death was not the end, so this new situation of life is not static. It is not hers to cling to and possess. She must let the Risen One have his own initiative, his own control. She has to learn not to obstruct the new movement in her eagerness to take hold of it. There are new ventures and new destinations for her newly restored master, which lie beyond her vision; she must allow freedom to the risen Son of God.

Jesus is disclosing himself so that his followers may understand that he is going to be with them as their ascended brother, truly alive but not physically visible. He is taking his human nature into the realm of the Father. Henceforth, our humanity is represented within the community of God; heaven will never be the same again. Henceforth, any insult to the humanity of any person, any treating of a human being as expendable rubbish, is strictly a blasphemy; it is an insult to the nature which God has eternally taken upon himself. Previously, Jesus has referred to his disciples as 'friends'. Now even this close and familiar term is insufficient. He has given them to each other as members of one family; now he stresses that he is in that family himself; he refers to them as 'my brothers'.

So Mary is sent off with a commission, a task to perform. She goes off to where the disciples are, and she has Jesus' message to pass on. She becomes an 'angel' to them, just as she has met with an 'angel' herself. She is an authentic apostle to those who are going to be apostles. Without her own story, she would merely be an uncommitted trafficker in information; without the commissioned word of Jesus, she would merely be a self-advertising freak. She tells what she has seen (with her understanding): she communicates Jesus' word.

Another model of the Easter experience is disclosed in the evening meeting of the disciple-group, where they have locked themselves in, fearful and anxious. Their purpose at this stage is merely to keep in touch with each other for their own self-interest and self-preservation. Christ, who has overcome the power of death, also defeats the bolts by which his followers seek to protect themselves. He comes like an expert burglar, and the first target for his skill in breaking and entering is the Church. The fears of the Church do not obstruct him. Naturally enough, the Church is scared to realize that its defences are so useless. But he overcomes this fear by his greeting of peace. And he convinces the disciples that they need not be afraid, by showing that he genuinely *is* the one who has been the victim of the cruelty of the cross.

The showing of the hands and side became a vital part of the Church's first preaching. The resurrection of Jesus was not just any resurrection. It was not just a sign that life is better than death, or that death is not the end. One day, perhaps, medical science might be able to bring a dead person back to life, but that would not be the same as the resurrection of Jesus. The resurrection of Jesus is not merely an event of super-advanced medical technology. It depends entirely on the fact that it is a *crucified* person who is resurrected. This man Jesus has been treated, carefully and precisely, as totally valueless and expendable. He has been given the treatment reserved by a counter-revolutionary state for the execution of convicted terrorists. No clearer way could have been found of saying that here is a person who is totally redundant, valueless and surplus to society's requirements.

The apostolic preaching is that God has made this Jesus both Lord and Christ; God has attributed supreme value to this man who was judged to be totally valueless by the tribunals of religion and state. It is the *Crucified One* who has been resurrected. The apostolic preaching goes on to say: If you are willing to recognize that your value systems have been totally faulty, if you want to make a new start, then come and join us; repent, take this new opportunity; be baptized, and share in the movement which represents this message of disturbance to the world. This is all represented by the clear demonstration that the Risen One remains the Crucified One. The meaning of crucifixion is not reversed or undone by the resurrection. The resurrection just makes clearer what was true all along in the programme of salvation in the cross.

Jesus shows his hands and his side. But his intention is not to rake up old grievances. There is no blame, no recrimination. Jesus treats his friends as if they are bursting with energy and enthusiasm for the next stage in history. He totally accepts them, as he has been accepted. So they can immediately be sent out with the same task and mandate he has been given: 'As the Father sent me, so I send you.' He makes explicit his dying act of handing over his Spirit. He shares his Spirit with them, so that they may become his new body. And he makes their mission and mandate explicit also. They are to make known the truth of forgiveness and to convince people of its validity. This is much more than a form of words. It is quite possible for the Church to give to people a formal assurance of forgiveness while keeping up a censorious or exclusive attitude towards those who are theoretically forgiven. The whole community is called to be an absolving, priestly community. It is in business to demonstrate that the inescapable link between offence and guilt has been broken, that the rigid barrier between the innocent and the guilty has been done away, that the most serious reason for barriers between person and person – the moral reason – has been replaced by a new principle of acceptance. The little community is sent into the world with this mandate and warning: if you communicate this forgiveness to people, they will genuinely be relieved of their guilt in the sight of God; if you fail to do so, there is no other resource for their healing.

The Church will often find itself in alliance with other interests and groups. It does not have a monopoly of goodness or justice or compassion or indignation. Along with others, it will expose, protest and criticize, and it will work with others in improving neighbourliness, justice and care. But the main and final mandate of the Church goes beyond what other agencies can undertake. Only the Church of Jesus has the symbols which make sense of this ultimate mandate, the mandate of forgiveness. When it acts on this mandate, it will often appear to be contradicting what it and its allies have been standing for.

Forgiveness often looks like compromise with unrighteousness, a loss of moral dignity. Forgiveness is the deliberate crossing of boundaries which moral society says should not be crossed. Jesus sends his Church to be like him, to knock away the convenient boundaries which good people draw. His offensive offends the world; a world which rejects forgiveness will find the Church offensive. A Church which contents itself with preserving the preciousness of the past will find the forgiving Church offensive. The forgiving Church stands for the power of God to bring transformation into a situation where we would prefer stability. We like to label people in terms of where they have come from, in terms of what they have done in the past. We are what we are because of what the past has made us. This is a basis of racism and elitism; it is also a basis of unforgivingness. We have labels to help us predict who are our friends and who are our enemies; we are thus defended against change and surprise. The risen Christ comes disturbing these predictabilities; he makes us what we can become. The New Covenant, like the Old, depends on God's power to release, to give wealth and land and knowledge back to those who have been in slavery, so that possession of them does not divide those who have from those who do not have. It creates a new community of hope, which is characteristically judged by how it relates to those who are strangers to it. All this is represented in the Risen One's creation of a new community of the freed, who are sent to take his freedom into his Father's world.

If forgiveness is not genuinely on offer, the best we can do is find someone to blame. We look around for someone who is obviously worthy of blame, and then load upon them the responsibility for all that has gone wrong. We Christians have set an example of this, over many centuries, by the way in which we have treated the Jews. This has given us good practice in the art of scapegoating; and now we apply this art to the homeless or the unemployed or the ethnic minorities. We make them carry the burden not only of their own disorder, but of ours, so that they are to blame for the prejudice which we feel against them. Those who operate this weapon of the blame-thrower become prosecuting counsel in their own cause. We urgently need to prove the other side wrong, and we ignore the evil in ourselves. We absolve the sins of the powerful – the strong, the manipulator, the bender of the system. This repression of guilt becomes a much more difficult disorder to tackle than straightforward guilt. It depends on untruth. The opposite of forgiveness is the lie. This is why the mandate of forgiveness is the necessary fulfilment of the whole process of the dying and rising of Jesus – Jesus the truth who comes to release us from the power of untruth. And this is why the Church has the continuing task of expressing God's forgiveness; this task is its constant godly protest against the false judgements of society; it will refuse to condone what the world wants it to condone, and it will absolve what the world wants it to condemn.

So we come to Thomas, the member of the disciple-community who was instinctively willing to die with Jesus. He is the one who stays away, who misses the party. Thomas is notorious as the doubter, but what exactly is it that he doubts? He does not doubt that Jesus is alive; if that were his problem, he could be convinced just by seeing Jesus or by grasping his arm. But he demands to make sure most specifically that this alive person has upon him the genuine marks of crucifixion. His anxiety, therefore, is not that the Risen One may turn out not to be really alive, but that he may turn out not truly to have died in the way that a crucified man dies. He is afraid that, after all, Jesus may turn out to be merely 'God', a supernatural being who could not really be hurt. If this were the case, then the whole previous experience of Jesus would be worthless. If Jesus is merely 'God' in disguise, or 'Godhead veiled in flesh', then he is a fraud and a disappointment on a cosmic scale. A risen 'God' is no use to struggling and suffering people; all he can do is to emphasize the eternal boundary between God and the human creature; the resurrection would then be a display of divine technology, which the human creature could admire but not share.

So Thomas insists on making sure that Jesus has been hurt as a human person would be hurt. Only if this is true is there any real miracle. But God has genuinely identified himself with humanity. God has become incarnate, and being incarnate means being at the mercy of the place where one is incarnated. The Risen One really has suffered; he has suffered not only the physical damage of spear and nails, but he has genuinely been crushed by the combined violence of a distorted religion, a penalizing state and a vicious public opinion. God has experienced complete redundancy and valuelessness. Thomas sees the scars with commitment, not just as a spectator. He needs nothing more.

The scars are the royal insignia of Jesus. When deaf people, for instance, wished to create a sign in sign language for 'Jesus', they could easily have based a sign on the existing signs for 'power', 'glory', 'king', 'lord' or 'leader', but they chose the scars; the sign for 'Jesus' is simply to point to the centre of the palm of each hand in turn. The scars show that there has been a genuine victory over death and over the powers of prejudice and unforgiveness, over all the destruction that can be caused by hatred and malice, over all the corrupted motives of religion and state and public opinion, which led to the death of the Son of God. The scars of Jesus show that this victory has been achieved in human experience, and that it is therefore a possibility for human beings to claim and experience it for themselves.

Thomas has insisted on seeing; so we have the final evidence that it is worthwhile to be human, that it is worthwhile to work for a society based on compassion and justice and forgiveness, in which people can grow in freedom and maturity; that it is worthwhile experiencing the pain caused by the informer, the betrayer, the denier, the religious prosecutor, the compromised judge, the perverted public voice. Only a genuine human being can present a valid crisis to other human beings. Only a genuine human being can expose other human beings' failure to be truly human, and can identify the motives of their inhumanity. Only a genuine human being can bear human vindictiveness and guilt; only a genuine human being can give a hope to be realized within this human world, rather than a hope of escaping from this world. This is what Thomas' doubt and hesitation stand for. He sees and believes.

So Thomas gives us the final clue to Easter. Easter is not just a fact of history, or a theory, or a general principle, or a doctrine. Easter is an exclamation, an overwhelming surprise. Easter is when you can see what your own humanity can be. Easter is when, face to face with a verifiably human being, you find yourself driven to cry, 'My Lord and my God.'

So the Evangelist has shown us the risen Christ

through the experience of four disciples, as varied and as different from each other as could be imagined. Our movement did not start in a tidy way. This is not what people could reasonably call 'organized religion'; resurrection faith is as disorganized a religion as we are ever likely to see. The people whom it touches are essentially various and diverse. There is no typical disciple and no typical resurrection experience. If there are any 'typical' Christians in our churches, they have to be very careful that they do not squeeze out the alternative Christians, the unusual, the misfits, the ones whose gifts the world will despise. All that the disciples have in common is Christ's gift and mandate of peace. This peace is not some inner tranquillity of the individual soul. It is the peace – in a full sense of the word, a 'political' peace – of a restored relationship with all that is outside oneself; it is peace with God; peace with the other disciple who is so different from oneself; peace with the other human being; peace with the creation of the Creator. The peace of Christ is a greeting, a gift and a task. It is the effect of resurrection. And if you ever want to find resurrection, you have to look for what has been crucified.

Thomas knows this. This is what he is looking for. And he sees it. But the last word is not with Thomas; it is with Jesus. Thomas believes because he sees. This is a blessing, but it is not a blessing which we can share. We do not see. The faith and the blessing which we can share is not that of Thomas, but of Jesus. It was because Jesus believed without seeing, it was because he remained committed in spite of certain failure, and was willing to make his own survival expendable, that there is a Gospel story to tell. We are not called to be the body of Thomas, but the body of Christ. We are called to share the role of the crucified, and this is impossible except to those who believe without seeing. Thomas is blessed, but the final blessing is upon those who have not seen and yet have believed.

What we have been told is sufficient for our task. The Evangelist knows that if his community of readers is to be the body of Christ, it will have to believe without seeing. Much more could have been told to us. Much that Jesus said and did has been left out and forgotten. But we do not need any more information about Jesus. Those first Christian communities had enough to enable them to be a witnessing community in which the dying and living of Christ was being worked out from day to day, and in a widening range of situations. Our knowledge of the story is due to the impact which it made on those who received the story at second hand, so that they saw fit to treasure and record it. We are alongside them as we read and listen.

So the story has come to us, and it is entrusted to us. We also are called to be a community which takes the crisis of Jesus into our present world. The truth of the dying and living of Jesus judges us and judges the world into which we are sent. Perhaps, within the limitations of our vision, it will still seem to us that we have a saviour who does not save, a king who does not rule, and a Christ who makes no observable difference to our destructive world. That would be a quite practical and realistic assessment. And then this Christ meets us, as we meet and recognize each other. If he is with us as the Risen One, he will be out of tune with all our ideas of what is possible and practicable. He will greet us with his peace, equip us with his peace and make us responsible for practising his peace. He will continue to treat us, in spite of our failures and fears, as his sisters and brothers, and as partners and representatives in his work. Our worship, then, will not be a device merely to recollect and to preserve something known and treasured from the past; it will not be a prescribed formula or an organized routine. At its heart our worship will be our exclamation of the surprise of Easter in the midst of our world – '*My Lord and my God*'.

For Group Work

General Questions

- How does this story fit into my experience?

- What bells does it ring for me?

- Have I ever been in the same situation as one of the characters in the story?

Specific Questions

1 Is your church primarily in business to preserve something or to bring in something new? What are the priorities suggested, for instance, by your church's financial accounts?

2 Look separately at the stories of four people in the stages of their journey into faith:

Mary Magdalene
Peter
the disciple whom Jesus loved
Thomas

Draw a line or graph to represent the ups and downs, the process of change, in the stories of these four people. Make a similar line or graph to represent your own journey. Which of the four are you most like? Is there room in your church for all these different kinds of people? Who are the misfits, the non-typical ones? Who has been squeezed out, or would not be able to squeeze in?

3 Where do you expect to find the risen Christ today? How will you recognize him? What are the 'scars' for you?

4 How is your church fulfilling Jesus' instruction to convey forgiveness to the world? How does this fit into your church's published programme?

At the end of your work as a group check back over the notes which you have been making, and see whether there are some insights or suggestions you may want to pass on to others – for instance, to your church leadership, to your local council, or to other groups in your area. As a result of your study, can you contribute to the worship and programme of your church over Good Friday and the Easter period?

For Prayer

Dialogue of the Son's Rising

People of God, why do you seek the living among the dead?

Because we are afraid; we are uncertain; we are poor and powerless, we want to hold on to what little we've got.

Do not be afraid; he has died; he lost all power; but he is with you as the sun is with you; He is the light ahead of you. People of God, why do you seek the living among the dead?

Because we are guilty; we shared in his killing; we didn't think he was worth standing up for. And now we're alone; and we're trying to save what we can from the wreckage.

Do not carry your guilt any longer. He has faced the worst that could be done to him. He has been treated as rubbish; he has been crushed by the best systems which people can invent; and he is stronger than the memories that trap and threaten you. He is free to be with you as the air is with you. He is the way ahead of you. People of God, why do you seek the living among the dead?

Because we want to be prudent; we want to be safe; we want to stay with what we're used to. Our world is being taken over by strangers. Our only security is the precious thing which we know.

You think you know about him?
You're sure you know where you put him?
You're confident you can find your way to the graveyard?
(Yes, of course, it's right next to the church, isn't it?)
Well, come;
Just come here;
Just come and see;
Just look at this empty hole . . .
People of God, you won't find him here;
You won't find him where you think you've got him.
He is risen. He is free.

So, he is risen;
So he is free.
So we are free.
But where is he now?

He is free.
He is on the road again.
But you can go too.
He shouted something over his shoulder, something like 'Catch me if you can.'

After him, then.

Yes, after him, People of God.
After him, and go with God.

Developed from 'Healings from the Empty Tomb' in
Norman Habel, *Interrobang*

Our Lord and our God, you are worthy
  to receive glory and honour and power.
You created all things,
  By your will they were made and were
  given life.
Christ, you are worthy,
  you were killed.
And by your blood you purchased people for God
  from every tribe and language and group
  and nation.
You have made us a royal house
  and a priestly community for our God.
To him who loves us,
  and frees us from our sin by his blood
be praise and honour
  glory and power, for ever and ever. Amen.

Acknowledgements

Chapter 1
Adaptation of a prayer by Eric Milner-White, from *A Procession of Passion Prayers*, SPCK, London, 1956.

'O Christ the Master Carpenter' by Arthur Gray, taken from *The Iona Community Worship Book*, Wild Goose Publications, Glasgow, 1991. Reproduced with permission.

Chapter 2
'Risen Jesus' by Brother Roger of Taizé, taken from *Praying Together in Word and Song – Taizé*, Mowbray, London, 1985. Copyright Ateliers et Presses de Taizé, 71250 Taizé Community, France.

Chapter 4
'Contemporary Reproaches' from 'Enemy of Apathy', *Wild Goose Songs Volume 2*, Wild Goose Publications, Glasgow, 1988. Words and music by John L Bell and Graham Maule. Copyright 1988 WGRG, Iona Community, 840 Govan Road, Glasgow G51 3UU, Scotland.

'Here hangs a man' from *Mainly Hymns*, Brian Wren, John Paul the Preacher's Press Leeds, 1980.

Chapter 5
'Behold the holy Lamb of God' (taken from *Cloth for the Cradle*, a cassette tape published by the Wild Goose Resource Group of the Iona Community, 1987), copyright Hope Publications, 380 South Main Place, Carol Stream, Illinois 60188, USA.

Chapter 6
'Dialogue of the Son's Rising' adapted from 'Healings from the Empty Tomb', *Interrobang*, Norman Habel, Fortress Press, Philadelphia, 1969.

Other books referred to
Lesslie Newbigin, *The Light Has Come*, Handsel Press, Edinburgh, 1982.
Stephen Verney, *Water Into Wine*, Collins Fount, London, 1985.
J C Fenton, *Preaching the Cross*, SPCK, London, 1958.
J C Fenton, *The Passion According to John*, SPCK, London, 1961.
John Davies, *Crisis*, The Christian Institute of South Africa, Johannesburg, 1969.